Decorations, Medals, Ribbons, Badges and Insignia of the United States Marine Corps

World War II to Present

By
James G. Thompson

1st Edition

This book is respectfully dedicated to the memory of
Cpl. Michael J. Banovez, Jr., USMC
M Company, 3rd Battalion, 5th Marines
Born Madison, Wisconsin, 1 July 1945
Died Chu Lai, Republic of Vietnam, 18 July 1966

"Semper Fi!"

Library of Congress Catalog Card Number - 97-071229
Hardcover Edition ISBN - 1-884452-39-6
Softcover Edition ISBN - 1-884452-38-8

Copyright 1998 by MOA Press

Published by:

MOA Press (Medals of America Press)
1929 Fairview Road
Fountain Inn, SC 29644-9137
Telephone: (864) 862-6051
HTTP://WWW.USMEDALS.COM

Printed in the United States of America

About the Author

James G. "Jim" Thompson

James G. "Jim" Thompson, graduated from the University of Wisconsin-Madison in 1960 and served as a regular officer in the United States Marine Corps from 1960 to 1964. His service included time as a Platoon Commander and Assistant S-4 in the 2nd Battalion, 2nd Marines, as well as Assistant S-4 for Embarkation on the staff of the 2nd Marines. He also served on sea duty as the Executive Officer of the Marine Detachment aboard the USS Randolph (CVS-15). Jim is a retired Sales Manager formerly with Procter & Gamble and resides with his wife Hannelore in Dunwoody, Georgia.

The photograph on the left was an official photograph of the author taken in the early 1960's; the one on the right was taken on the parade deck at MCRD, Parris Island, where Jim had the pleasure of watching his son Dan follow in the family tradition.

Grateful Acknowledgments

Headquarters, United States Marine Corps
Major A. E. "Betsy" Arends, USMC - Special Assistant
   to the Commandant for Public Affairs

United States Marine Corps - Awards Branch
Colonel Fred Anthony, USMC Ret. - Director
Mrs. Charlene Rose - Assistant Director

Marine Historical Center
Mr. Benis M. Frank - Chief Historian of the Marine Corps
Mr. Danny J. Crawford - Head, Reference Section
Mr. Robert V. Aquilina - Assistant Head, Reference Section
Lieutenant Colonel Charles V. Mugno, USMC -
   Museum Volunteer

Marine Corps Art Collection
Lieutenant Colonel Donna J. Neary, USMCR - Artist

Marine Corps Museums Branch
Mr. Kenneth L. Smith-Christmas - Curator, Material History
Mrs. Nancy King - Uniform Specialist

4th Marine Air Wing
Lieutenant Colonel Jeffrey J. Douglass, USMCR - Public
   Affairs Officer, MAG 42

Marine Corps Logistics Data Management Center
Master Sergeant Robert G. McCormick, USMC Ret. -
   Equipment Specialist

Institute of Heraldry, United States Army
Colonel Gerald T. Luchino, USA Ret. - former Director
Mr. Thomas B. Profitt - Director

Young Marines of the Marine Corps League
Mr. Jim Parker - Administrator

Medals of America, Inc.
Mrs. Linda Foster - President
Colonel Frank Foster, USA Ret.
Lieutenant Lee Foster, US Army National Guard
Lieutenant Colonel Anthony Aldebol, USAF Ret.
Mrs. Bonnie Crocker
First Sergeant Barbara Wamsley, USMC Ret.

Others
General Walter E. Boomer, USMC Ret. - former Assistant
   Commandant
Mr. Lawrence H. Borts - Author and Consultant
Mr. John Jones - former Captain, USMCR and Naval
   Aviator
Mr. William M. Schneider - former Gunnery Sergeant,
   USMC and Collector
Mr. Ted A. Thurman - Shoulder Patches
Mr. J.L. Morgan - Shoulder Patches
Mr. Duane Neyens - Shoulder Patches
Mrs. Hannelore Thompson - supportive wife and diligent
   proof reader

General Walter E. Boomer
*Former Assistant Commandant
and
CG Marine Forces Central Command,
1ˢᵗ Marine Expeditionary Force,
Desert Storm*

"I wondered why Jim Thompson called and asked me to write a fore-
word for this book. First, I hadn't seen Jim over 30 years and second, I
wondered if there was really a need for such a book. After speaking with
Jim and learning of his enduring love for the Corps, I understood why he
was talked into such an undertaking. After seeing the draft of the book, I
appreciated how such a volume might be useful to Marines. I remembered
from my own service, that information on decorations and medals and
ribbons never seemed to be found in one place. This concise little book
puts it all together for you. Equally important it is done with Marines
specifically in mind. Jim has done Marines an excellent service."

— General Walter E. Boomer, USMC, Retired

Table of Contents

List of Illustrations

Last year, while contemplating retirement from a career of 32 years with Procter & Gamble, I was approached by an old friend, who is in the publishing business, with the suggestion that I write a reference book on the badges and decorations of the Marine Corps. At first I was puzzled as to why he had asked me, even though he knew that I had served for four years as a regular officer and loved the Corps. His intent was to convince me that my love for the Corps should be sufficient reason to take on the job. In addition, he believed that there was a need for such a book. Still doubtful, I argued that there must be many books available on this subject, so why should I do a "me too" book. He asked me to prove the validity of my objection to myself by researching Bowker's "Books in Print" and "Baker and Taylor" to find out what books were currently available on the subject. Following his suggestion, I learned, to my surprise, that although there were books about military insignia and books on U.S. decorations, there was little or nothing in print on these subjects devoted specifically to the Marine Corps. With this realization and a little more coaxing I decided to write this book.

This book is designed to be a definitive reference covering Marine Corps decorations, medals, ribbons, badges and insignia since World War II. The book is written for Marines: Marines on active duty, Marine veterans, and those who are interested in Marines. The book is intended to be a single source on these subjects and detailed enough to meet the needs of historians and collectors. Material for this book was derived from many authoritative sources, but the most valuable information came from the Marine Corps itself: Fellow Marines, The Marine Corps Historical Center, The Marine Corps Awards Branch and The Marine Corps Museum. Portions of this book were taken directly from the current Marine Corps Uniform Regulations to insure accuracy.

This book, like all reference books, is out of date almost as soon as it is published. In the area of decorations, changes are being made constantly. For example, there have been eighty-one new U.S. decorations created since 1947, or an average of over $1\frac{1}{2}$ new awards a year. Although the Marine Corps has had fewer changes than other services since World War II, it too, is difficult to stay current with.

As with any book there are bound to be mistakes. If errors are detected, please accept my apologies and the assurance that they will be rectified in future editions. Factual errors will also be found in this book and I encourage those of you seeking the ultimate in accuracy to communicate corrections to me through the publisher, or directly. As a Marine, it is my sincere hope that this book and the facts it contains be an accurate reference work and a credit to the Corps.

The history and tradition of the United States Marine Corps, its decorations, medals, ribbons, badges and insignia are a part of what makes the Corps what it is. The Corps has a rich tradition of symbols; these bits of metal, cloth and ribbon add special character, and this book, in a small way, is intended to provide good reference to this end.

Jim Thompson
Dunwoody, Georgia

The decorations of the late Cpl. Michael J. Banovez, Jr., USMC, to whom this book is dedicated.

Background and History

The Continental Marines were established by resolution of the Second Continental Congress on 10 November 1775. The resolution called for the recruitment of two battalions. The uniform of the Continental Marines was a green cutaway coat with either white or scarlet facings and waistcoat, light colored breeches, wool stockings with black gaiters, a round black hat with white trim and a leather neck stock. Since this first "uniform regulation," there have been many changes in the uniforms, the decorations, the medals, the ribbons, the badges and the insignia of the Corps. This brief background and history will touch on just a few.

After the War for Independence the Marine Corps went out of existence until reorganized in 1798. On 11 July of that year, President John Adams signed into law "An Act for Establishing and Organizing a Marine Corps," authorizing 33 officers and 848 men. During this period through the War of 1812, Marines were dressed in blue tailcoats edged with red, white breeches and cross belts and high shakos. By the 1820's uniforms became very ornamental with coats trimmed in gold lace and headdress plumes. In 1852 the traditional red stripe reappeared on the uniform trousers of officers and noncommissioned officers.

Quatrefoil

The quatrefoil (cross-shaped braid) first appeared on the top of Marine officers' caps in 1859 and has been a part of the officers' uniforms ever since.

Civil War Era Insignia

Uniforms during the Civil War period were similar to that of the Army infantry with dark blue coats and light blue trousers (with the red stripe). During this period the Marine cap insignia took the form of the light infantry horn with the letter "M" in the loop.

Early Insignia

In 1868, the eagle, globe and anchor were adopted as the new emblem of the Marine Corps. In the 1870's, the Marine uniform was standardized and 1900 marked the end of colorful uniforms, except for dress. The turn of the century also brought about the use of marksmanship badges emphasizing the importance of skill with weapons to the mission of the Corps.

Early Marksmanship Badges

During World War I Marines wore khaki colored uniforms, traded in their field hats for overseas caps and wore steel helmets in combat for the first time. Shoulder insignia also appeared for the first time on the uniforms of the 4th and 5th Brigades. After the fighting at Belleau Wood, Secretary of the Navy Franklin D. Roosevelt directed that uniform regulations be changed, authorizing Marine enlisted personnel to wear the Corps' emblem on their collars. Also during World War I, a grateful French Government awarded the Fourragere, a braided cord symbolizing bravery in battle, to the 5th and 6th Marine Regiments. German soldiers encountering Marines during this period referred to them as "Teufelshunden" (devil dogs).

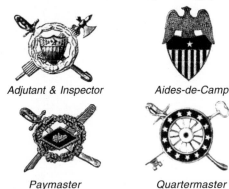

Adjutant & Inspector   *Aides-de-Camp*

Paymaster   *Quartermaster*

During the period between the World Wars, the size of the Corps was reduced significantly and there were few changes made in the uniform. During this period specialty insignia were worn by officers and enlisted personnel. These insignia were worn by the Adjutant and Inspector's Department, the Paymaster's Department, the Quartermaster's Department and generals' aides-de-camp. Officers wore them on coat lapels below the Marine Corps insignia, or to the rear of the insignia on standing collars. Pay clerks and quartermaster clerks wore their devices on their collars. These insignia were bronze on greens and khaki, and gilt/enameled on blues. The practice of wearing specialty insignia was abolished in 1943.

WW II Shoulder Insignia

World War II brought the use of dungarees, or utilities, for field wear along with a new, more functional steel helmet, and shoulder insignia (shoulder patches) reappeared on the service uniform. During the war Marines were committed to the taking of islands in the Pacific. In the Central Pacific, in 1943, the camouflage helmet cover was instituted and became a trademark of Marines in combat. From the time of Guadalcanal to Okinawa there was little use for dress uniforms, but the use of awards and decorations to recognize units and Marines was in "full swing." The use of shoulder insignia ended shortly following the war.

On 12 June 1948, Congress passed the Women's Armed Forces Integration Act, which authorized the acceptance of women into the Regular component of the Marine Corps. Uniforms and insignia for Women Marines have been similar to those of their male counterparts from their inception.

The 1950's and the Korean War brought about few changes in the Marine uniform, but this period saw the advent of foreign campaign decorations as well as United Nations recognition. During the "Conflict," Marines, on the ground, were assigned missions similar to Army units and aviation elements were placed under the control of the Air Force. It was during this period that the Marine Corps had to fight fiercely to maintain its identity.

WW II - Korea   *1959-Present*

The twentieth century saw many changes in the enlisted rank structure and 1959 was no exception. The change in 1959 saw the old Lance Corporal rank reinstated, as well as providing two new pay grades (E-8 and E-9) for senior staff NCO's (first sergeant/master sergeant and sergeant major/master gunnery sergeant). Interestingly, neither the officers nor enlisted rank structure has significantly changed since the sixties. The notable exceptions can be found within the warrant officer ranks and the addition of the general officer rank (four stars) for the Commandant and Assistant Commandant.

In January 1974, the summer service khaki uniform was replaced by a light weight green service uniform, so that now Marines are seen in "Marine green" the year round. Although there were few changes in Marine uniforms or insignia since Vietnam, the number of new campaign medals and foreign decorations continues to grow with the Corps' involvement throughout the world.

Decorations, Medals and Ribbons — Napoleon wrote, " A soldier will fight long and well for a bit of colored ribbon." Wellington, Napoleon's conqueror, introduced campaign medals to the British Army and the first went to troops who defeated Napoleon at Waterloo. Both Napoleon and Wellington realized that decorations and medals express national gratitude and stimulate esprit de corps.

The history of military decorations in the United States began early in the American Revolution, when Congress voted to award gold medals to outstanding military leaders. The first medal was struck to honor George Washington for his service in driving the British from Boston in 1776. Similar medals were awarded to General Horatio Gates for his victory at the Battle of Saratoga and Captain John Paul Jones after his famous naval engagement with the Serapis in 1779. Unlike present practice, however, these were large presentation medals not designed to be worn on a uniform.

The Andre Medal

In 1780, the Congress of the United States created the Andre Medal, which, for the first time, broke the custom of restricting the awarding of medals to senior officers. It is doubly unique in that it was designed to be worn with the uniform as a neck decoration. The medal was awarded to three enlisted men who captured Major John Andre who had the plans of the West Point fortification in his boot. The medal commemorated the fidelity and patriotism of these three men.

Purple Heart

In 1782, George Washington established the Badge of Military Merit, the first U.S. decoration that had general application to all enlisted men and was the forerunner of the Purple Heart. Washington hoped that this would inaugurate a permanent awards system. Although special and commemorative medals had been awarded previously, until this point no decoration had been established which honored the private soldier with an award of special merit. The object of the Badge of Military Merit was "to foster and encourage every species of military merit." The medal was a heart of purple cloth or silk, edged with narrow lace or binding. Unfortunately, the award fell into disuse after the Revolution and disappeared for 150 years.

On the 200th anniversary of Washington's birth, 22 February 1932, the Badge of Military merit was reborn as the Purple Heart. The Purple Heart took the heart shape of the earlier Badge of Military Merit with Washington's profile on a purple background. The words "For Military Merit" appear on the reverse in reference to its predecessor.

1861 Navy Medal of Honor

During the Civil War the Medal of Honor was established and remained the only American military award until the Marine Corps authorized the Good Conduct Medal in 1896. It was not until the eve of the 20th Century that seven medals were authorized to commemorate the events surrounding the Spanish American War. One of these medals was to commemorate the victory of the naval forces under Commodore Dewey over the Spanish fleet at Manila Bay. This medal was awarded to all officers and enlisted personnel present during the expedition and became this Country's first campaign medal.

When Theodore Roosevelt became President, he legislated the creation of medals to honor all those who

had served in previous conflicts. By 1908, the United States had authorized campaign medals, some retroactive, for the Civil War, the Indian Wars, the Spanish American War, the Philippine Insurrection and the China Relief Expedition of 1900-01. The Services used the same ribbon, but different medals were struck for the Army and Navy. The custom of wearing the ribbons of the medals on a ribbon bar began during this period. The Army and the Navy used different precedence for wearing these ribbons, which established an independence in the creation and wearing of awards by each service that remains to this day.

Army Distinguished Service Cross   *Navy Cross*

At the time of the U.S. entry into World War I, the Medal of Honor, Certificate of Merit and the Navy/Marine Good Conduct Medals were the only personal decorations. In 1918, the Army's Distinguished Service Cross and Navy Distinguished Service Medal were established. That same year, the law which prevented individuals from accepting foreign decorations, was rescinded. In 1919, the Navy created the Navy Cross and the Distinguished Service Medal for Navy and Marine personnel. The issuance of the Sampson Medal in 1898 established the practice of wearing clasps with the names of battles on the suspension ribbon, which was a practice in many countries.

Brevet Medal

In 1921, the Secretary of the Navy authorized the Brevet Medal for 20 officers whose commissions had been approved by Congress. Major General John A. Lejeune (Commandant of the Marine Corps 1920-29) felt that living officers who had received brevet commissions between 1861 and 1915 should receive a medal, in addition to their commissions, as a reward for heroism. This rarest of all U.S. decorations was already obsolete by the time it was approved. The Brevet commission lapsed into disuse in 1921.

On 8 September 1939, President Franklin Roosevelt proclaimed a National Emergency and the first peacetime service award, the American Defense Service Medal, was established. At the beginning of World War II the United States increased the number of personal decorations as well as campaign medals. Since U.S. forces were serving all over the world, a campaign medal was established for each major theater. The three medals were American Campaign, Asiatic-Pacific Campaign and European-African-Middle Eastern Campaign. The World War I practice of using clasps to denote campaigns on the suspension ribbon was discarded in favor of three-sixteenth inch bronze stars.

Following World War II, the World War II Victory Medal and the Occupation Medals (for both Europe and Japan) were authorized. During the Korean Conflict the Korean Service Medal and the United Nations Service Medal were established along with the National Defense Service Medal. The National Defense Service Medal was also instituted during the Korean Conflict and later became our Country's most awarded medal when it was reinstated for the Vietnam and Gulf Wars.

The first American Advisors in the Republic of South

Vietnam were awarded the new Armed Forces Expeditionary Medal created in 1961 to cover campaigns for which no specific medal was instituted. As U.S. involvement in Southeast Asia grew, the Vietnam Service Medal was authorized. Uniquely, the previous recipients of the Expeditionary medal were given the opportunity to decide which award to accept. The Department of Defense also authorized the acceptance of the Republic of Vietnam Campaign Medal by all who served six months in-country or in the surrounding waters from July 1965 to March 1973.

During the Vietnam era, and immediately following, the Department of Defense developed several new decorations including the Defense Distinguished Service Medal, the Defense Superior Service Medal and the Defense Meritorious Service Medal. Each of these awards was designed to recognize achievements of individuals assigned to the Office of the Secretary of Defense or other activities in the Department of Defense.

The Gulf War saw the reinstatement of the National Defense Service Medal (this time it also included the Reserves) and the creation of the Southwest Asia Service Medal. The Department of Defense also approved the acceptance and wearing of the Kuwait Liberation Medal s awarded by Saudi Arabia and the Emirate of Kuwait.

During the 1990's many Marines were awarded the NATO (North Atlantic Treaty Organization) Medal for service under NATO command or in direct support of NATO operations.

In 1995, the Marine Corps established the Marine Corps Recruiting Ribbon, and, in 1997, the Commandant approved the new Marine Corps Drill Instructor Ribbon and Marine Security Guard Ribbon.

Badges and Insignia — Insignia of one kind or another have been worn or displayed since the beginning of time. Prehistoric tribes were known by their emblems; the eagle, the bear and the fox are but a few examples. Knights in the Middle Ages could be recognized by the designs on their shields or the crests on their helmets. In modern times, clubs and fraternities have their pins and badges, and every state and nation has its seal and flag. Insignia of many kinds are used by all the Armed Forces. They show service, rank, and, in the case of the Army, job assignment and unit.

One important purpose of military insignia is to show the wearer's rank. At the beginning of the War for Independence, General Washington's non commissioned officers sewed strips of cloth to their right shoulders to help soldiers recognize their leaders. During this period officers of the Continental Army wore different colored cockades on their hats to signify rank.

Throughout the years the Marine Corps, like the Army, gradually developed the symbols of rank. Officers at different times wore fringed shoulder decorations called epaulets, then shoulder knots, then shoulder straps, and finally the metal insignia we know today. The stars used by general officers date from 1780, the eagles worn by colonels date from 1832, and the leaves and bars from 1836. Most of these symbols are well known in heraldry; the stars indicate a high or controlling position; the eagle is patterned on the American eagle, well known for its courage and commanding appearance; the oak leaf is a symbol of strength, and the lieutenants' bars are much like those used on knights' shields.

The chevron has changed in size and shape over the years, but has been the insignia of enlisted rank since the 1840's. The chevron is an ancient emblem and has roots in the middle ages. Some say that chevrons were awarded to a knight for placement on his shield to show that he had taken part in capturing a castle, town or other fortification, of which the chevron resembled the roof.

History leaves much to the imagination regarding the origin and significance of the devices or distinguishing insignia of the Marine Corps. However, it is known that since 1740, when the first American Marines served under the British flag, Marines have always had some insignia, badge, mark, device, or ornament of distinguishment.

The first written authorization on Marine uniforms is in the "Minutes of the Marine Committee of the Continental Congress for 5 September 1776". The Continental Marines, not yet officially a Corps, first wore a green coat. The "green" coat was, by itself, distinctive. These first United States Marines also wore a leather stock around their neck (as did the Army). This uniform item led to the nickname "Leatherneck" and became a mark of distinction and one of the first unofficial insignias of the Corps.

In the years following the Revolution, Marines had little to distinguish themselves from the Army and even had to wear surplus Army uniforms. During this period, there were numerous distinguishing marks prescribed such as black cockades, buck tails, brass plates, yellow bands and tassels and cap plates.

Early Enlisted Shako Plate

In the early 1800's, the Marine Corps adopted a new uniform consisting of a dark blue coat with scarlet facings and gold trim and white trousers. The new uniform also had a tall, black, stiff-crowned cap (or shako) with a brass plate on the front with the word "MARINES" spelled out in half-inch letters across the bottom.

In 1804, the Marine uniform button displayed an eagle perched upon a fouled anchor surrounded by thirteen six pointed stars. Later the stars were changed from six pointed to five pointed stars and the button has been used by the Corps with only minor changes ever since. As a point of interest, this device is the oldest military insignia in continuous use in the United States.

During the War of 1812, the uniform changed little except that the officers' headgear had evolved to a fore-and-aft cocked hat with a gold American eagle on the left side. In 1820, the uniform changed and a brass American eagle appeared on the dark blue bell-crowned dress shako for junior officers and enlisted.

1830's Enlisted Cap Badge

On 4 November 1834, Marines were directed to wear a brass eagle on the covers, and that officers wear the letters "M.C." on their epaulets. In 1840, the undress uniform cap had a gold wreath, possibly taken from the laurel wreath of the Royal Marine emblem, encircling the letters. "U.S.M." In 1845, a fouled anchor and wreath was prescribed for officers in place of the letters "U.S.M."

1859-76 Officer's Full Dress Cap Insignia

The Civil War period saw the Marine insignia evolve into the light infantry horn or bugle with the letter "M" inside the ring of the horn to signify Marine. The full dress insignia from 1859 to 1868 was a gold infantry bugle with a silver letter "M" on large gold U.S. shield resting on a half wreath.

It wasn't until 1868 that the current emblem was adopted. The Emblem was designed by Brigadier General Jacob Zeilin, the 7th Commandant. General Zeilin felt that there was a need for a more distinctive emblem than the infantry bugle with the letter "M", which had been in use since 1859.

Early Royal Marine Emblem

General Zeilin wrote to the Secretary of the Navy: *"The Marine Corps of the United States was organized after that of the Royal Marines of Great Britain - a Corps of over two hundred years eminently distinguished for its service on land as well as for its legitimate duty with the Navy. The proud motto of this Royal Corps, 'Per Mare, per Terram,' so well known all over the world, was authorized by the Navy Department to be placed on the flag of the United States Marine Corps in English words, 'By Sea and Land' in commemoration of our service with the Army in the field during the war with Mexico..."*

1876-92 Officer's Full Dress Cap Insignia

In view of this letter, which clearly indicates that the U. S. Marine Corps was modeled after the Royal Marines,

it is believed that the U. S. Marine Corps emblem was taken directly from the Royal Marine emblem (the Globe and Laurel). The globe was used as the centerpiece, but employing the projection of the Western Hemisphere rather than the Eastern. The hemisphere is surmounted by a spread eagle rather than the crown. Although no particular eagle was specified in the original design, it has been surmised that the eagle is a crested eagle based on the idea that the Marine Corps covered the whole world and that the crested eagle would be more symbolic than the American bald eagle. The fouled anchor, similar to the one on the Royal Marine emblem, was used in the design, since it had been used in several early U.S. Marine emblems and also showed the Corps to be maritime. Although the "fouled anchor" does not suggest good seamanship, this fouled anchor design, the badge of the British Lord High Admiral, was first ordered in 1747 for the Royal Marines as an honor. The insignia for the dress uniform shako during this period employed the eagle, globe and anchor on a gold U.S. shield.

1870's Dress Helmet Insignia

In the late 1800's, the Corps adopted a large gold Marine Corps emblem as an insignia for a spiked dress helmet. The eagle for this insignia was very pronounced with a large wing span (2 ½ inches across). The Spanish American War in 1898 and the Boxer Rebellion in 1900 saw the insignia evolve into the shape and size as worn today. Over the years the insignia experienced minor variations in design and so the Commandant and the Acting Secretary of the Navy approved an "official" design on 28 May 1925. The current insignia was standardized in 1936.

1936 Emblem Design

Whether a Marine is a general or a private is secondary to the privilege he or she shares in wearing the Emblem. The Eagle, Globe and Anchor is the most important insignia of the Corps.

Marine Corps Insignia

The Marine Corps has great respect for everything and anything that enhances the uniqueness of the Corps and fosters the discipline, loyalty, courage, brotherhood and achievement that make the word "Marine"…stand for the highest definition of military pride. The insignia of the Marine Corps are very much a part of this pride on display.

Marine Corps Emblem - displays an eagle above a globe of the Western Hemisphere backed by a fouled anchor. In the eagle's beak is a scroll emblazoned with the Latin motto of the Corps, *Semper Fidelis (Always Faithful)*.

The Emblem of the Marine Corps was adopted in 1868 and was designed by the Brigadier General Jacob Zeilin, the 7th Commandant.

Official Seal of the Marine Corps - consists of the traditional bronze Marine Corps Emblem, which is displayed on a scarlet background. The emblem is encircled with a navy blue band edged in a gold rope rim and inscribed Department of the Navy, United States Marine Corps in gold letters.

The Official Seal of the Marine Corps was established on 22 June 1954 and was designed by General Lemuel C. Shepherd, Jr., the 20th Commandant.

Branch of Service Insignia - is modeled after the Marine Corps Emblem, except without the motto scroll. This insignia is worn on the uniform cap, coat collars and lapels. The officers' dress insignia is gold and silver. The enlisted branch of service insignia is the same general design as the officers' insignia except the dress insignia is gold. The service insignia was bronze from World War II until June 1963 when the color was changed to non-glossy black. The service insignia for both officers and enlisted is currently non-glossy black.

Interestingly, officers have worn the insignia on their collars since the 1870's, but enlisted Marines didn't have this privilege until World War I, when Franklin D. Roosevelt, as Secretary of the Navy, directed them to wear insignia discs. This change was in recognition of the 4th Marine Brigade's victory at Belleau Wood. The eagle, globe and anchor insignia was approved for enlisted Marines in 1920. From 1941 to 1961 the collar device was also worn on the enlisted shirt collars (when coats were not worn). Also during this period the anchor on the insignia was not fouled with anchor cable.

Since the current insignia was standardized in 1936, manufacturers of Marine Corps insignia have been held to very tight contract specifications. There have been no changes in the current design for enlisted insignia since 1956 and officers since 1962. Marines refer to the insignia as the "Bird and Ball", or the "Globe and Anchor", but it is more properly called the "Eagle, Globe and Anchor."

The current officers' branch of service insignia for the dress/service cap consists of a view of the globe (Western Hemisphere) about 7/8 inch in diameter, intersected by a fouled anchor, and surmounted by an eagle. The rope of the fouled anchor is only connected at distinct points. The insignia is provided with a screwpost securely soldered to and projecting from the approximate center rear of the globe, and fitted with a milled nut. The dress insignia is gold and silver while the service insignia is finished in non-glossy black.

The design of the current officers' dress collar insignia is identical to the dress cap insignia, except that it is about 11/16 inch in diameter.

The design of the officers' service collar insignia is identical to the service cap insignia, except that it is 9/16 inch in diameter.

Enlisted branch of service insignia is the same general design as officers' insignia, except that the rope is continuously connected to the fouled anchor of the emblem. Dress insignia is stamped of gold color metal while service insignia is stamped and finished in non-glossy black.

Uniform Buttons - come in gold and non glossy-black. The buttons display an eagle perched on top of a fouled anchor and thirteen stars surround the upper edge. The dress buttons are gold with a burnished rim, while the service uniform buttons are non-glossy black.

Necktie (field scarf) Clasp - is a lined stamped gold bar with a Marine Corps emblem on a centered gold disc; the officers' clasp has the emblem in silver, while the enlisted clasp has a gold emblem. The original clasp, worn in the mid to late '50's by both officers and enlisted, was non-glossy black.

During the Vietnam period, as the width of civilian neckties narrowed, so did the width of the field scarf and the necktie clasp. No necktie clasp was worn During World War II and immediately following.

Honorable Service Lapel Pin (World War II Honorable Discharge Pin) - was a token of appreciation given to every American service member who was discharged during and after World War II for service between September 1939 and December 1946. The pin is a small gold-plated brass emblem 7/16 inches high by 5/8 inches wide. This "Badge of Service," nicknamed "Ruptured Duck," was designed by Anthony de Franisci for the War Department. The design consists of an eagle perched within a ring and is worn as a civilian suit lapel button. This same design was used as a cloth insignia (1-1/2 inches high by 3 inches wide for wear on the uniform) for all Marines who were permitted to wear their uniform after being discharged.

Honorable Discharge Lapel Pin - is a small gold-plated brass emblem 7/16 inches high by 5/8 inches wide.

The design consists of a Marine Corps emblem in a circle with the words U.S. Marine Corps - Honorable Discharge. This pin is intended to be worn as a civilian suit lapel pin.

Retirement Lapel Pin - is a small plated emblem 7/16 inches high by 5/8 inches wide. The design consists of a Marine Corps emblem in a circle with the words U.S. Marine Corps - Retired. The pin is gold for twenty years service and silver for thirty. This pin is intended to be worn as a civilian suit lapel pin.

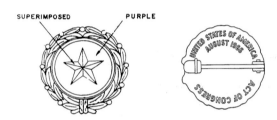

Gold Star Pin - is a small gold-plated brass emblem 7/16 inches high by 5/8 inches wide. The design consists of a gold star encircled by a laurel wreath. This pin is presented to the families of Marines killed in the line of duty and is intended to be worn as recognition of the appreciation of a grateful nation. The pin is also known as the "Gold Star Mothers" pin.

Officer Candidate Program Insignia - During World War II, and the two decades following, Marine Officer Candidates wore collar insignia identifying them as Officer Candidates (OC), Platoon Leaders Class (PLC) and Marine Air Cadets (MARCAD). Officer Candidates wore silver "OC" insignia; Platoon Leaders Class Candidates wore gold (Class 1) and silver (Class 2) "PLC" insignia; and Marine Aviation Cadets wore gold winged silver propellers. Marine Option NROTC Midshipmen wore no identifying collar insignia.

Navy Insignia

The Marine Corps, being a part of the Department of the Navy, receives its medical, dental and religious support from the Navy.

Hospital Corpsman

Religious Program Specialist

Dental Technician

Petty Officer 1st class

Petty Officer 2nd class

Petty Officer 3rd class

Enlisted Navy personnel attached to the Corps providing these services are authorized to wear Marine Corps service and utility uniforms, but wear their rank and corps insignia. On the service uniform the Navy rank and corps insignia is black on green.

Chaplains

Christian   Jewish   Buddhist   Muslim

Chaplains, medical and dental officers are also authorized to wear Marine Corps utility uniforms with their appropriate rank and corps insignia when serving with Marine units.

Medical   Dental

Flight Surgeon

Navy medical officers also serve Marine Air Wings as flight surgeons.

"Seabee"

Naval Construction Battalions served with the Corps during the Pacific Campaigns of World War II. These "Seabees" often fought side by side with Marines building airfields and support facilities.

Eur.-African-Mid. East Campaign Medal

Asiatic-Pacific Campaign Medal

Korean Service Medal

Armed Forces Expeditionary Medal

Vietnam Service Medal

Southwest Asia Service Medal

Navy personnel have served gallantly with the Corps over the years and are a part of its proud history. Those attached to the Corps during campaigns of World War II, Korea, Vietnam, and Southwest Asia are entitled to wear a small Marine Corps emblem device on the ribbon of the appropriate campaign medal.

Officer Cap Insignia

Chief Petty Officer Cap Insignia

1970's Enlisted Cap Insignia
(still worn by female enlisted personnel)

Breast insignia are worn by Marines who are qualified/designated in selected areas. Breast insignia are worn on the left breast of all service and dress coats, and may be worn on khaki shirts or utility jackets when worn as an outer garment. Not more than two Marine Corps approved breast insignia are worn on the left, and not more than one foreign pilot or other U.S. service pilot /navigator insignia is worn on the right at a time. Miniature insignia, one-half regular size, are worn on evening dress jackets.

Naval Aviator Insignia - Bronze, gold-plated metal pin consisting of a fouled anchor surmounted by a shield, centered on the basic wings. The fouled anchor is 7/8 inch long. The height and width of the shield is 1/2 inch. The Naval Aviator Insignia is awarded to officers who have successfully completed an authorized course of instruction (Naval Flight School-Pensacola) as prescribed by the Commandant of the Marine Corps (CMC) or the Chief of Naval Operations (CNO).

Naval Flight Officer Insignia - Bronze, gold-plated metal pin consisting of two crossed fouled anchors surcharged with a shield, centered on the basic wings. The fouled anchors are 7/8 inch long. The height and width of the shield is 1/2 inch. The Naval Flight Officer Insignia is awarded to officers who have successfully completed an appropriate course of instruction as prescribed by the Commandant of the Marine Corps (CMC) or the Chief of Naval Operations (CNO).

Naval Astronaut Insignia - Bronze, gold-plated wings of a Naval Aviator or Naval Flight Officer with a shooting star and ring superimposed upon the center shield (see page 51). A Marine designated by the CMC as a Naval Astronaut (pilot, NFO, or mission specialist) wears the Naval Astronaut Insignia.

Marine Aerial Navigator Insignia - Bronze, gold-plated metal pin consisting of the basic wings with a central device of two fouled anchors surmounted by a replica of a mariner's compass, superimposed on a silver-colored disk. The fouled anchors are 5/8 inch long; diameter of the disk, 1/2 inch; diameter of the compass, 3/8 inch. The Marine Aerial Navigator Insignia is awarded to Marine officers and enlisted personnel who have successfully completed an appropriate course of instruction as prescribed by the Military Occupational Specialty (MOS) manual. The Insignia was instituted in 1945 as the "Naval Aviation Observers (Navigation) Insignia."

Naval Aviation Observer Insignia - Bronze, gold-plated metal pin consisting of the basic wings with a central device of an "O" circumscribing an erect plain anchor, both in silver in bold relief, the center of the "O" being filled with gold. The outer diameter of the "O" is 3/4 inch; inner diameter, 9/16 inch; height of the anchor, 1/2 inch. The Naval Aviation Observer Insignia is awarded to individuals who have successfully completed an appropriate course of instruction as prescribed by Headquarters Marine Corps (HQMC) and accumulated 200 hours of flight time directly related to the specified aerial duty. At one time this insignia was also awarded to Marines who are now authorized to wear the Naval Aircrew Insignia.

Naval Aviation Observer (Tactical) Insignia (Obsolete) - Bronze, gold-plated metal pin consisting of basic wings with a silver centerpiece superimposed upon two gold crossed fouled anchors. The silver centerpiece device has two crossed guns (naval rifles) superimposed upon it in bold relief and in gold color. The insignia measures 2 ¾ inches from wingtip to wingtip. The Naval Aviation Observers (Tactical) Insignia was established in February 1946 for commissioned officers and warrant officers of the Navy and Marine Corps who performed duties as gunfire spotters, artillery spotters, and general liaison and observing duties in connection with amphibious operations. The insignia was awarded to officers who completed the "Basic Course" at Air Observers School and accumulated one hundred hours flying time as an aerial observer. This insignia became obsolete on 18 March 1947 and has been replaced by the current Naval Aviation Observer Insignia.

Naval Aviation Observer (Radar) Insignia (Obsolete) - Bronze, gold-plated metal pin consisting of basic wings with a silver centerpiece superimposed upon two gold crossed fouled anchors. The silver centerpiece device has a symbolic radar manifestation in gold bold relief superimposed upon it. The insignia measures 2 ¾ inches from wingtip to wingtip. The Naval Aviation Observers (Radar) Insignia was established in October 1945. This insignia was worn by Naval Aviation Observers (Radar) and enlisted Aviation Radar-Navigators designated by Headquarters Marine Corps. This insignia became obsolete on 18 March 1947.

Balloon Pilot Insignia - Bronze, gold-plated metal pin consisting of a fouled anchor surmounted by a shield, centered on half of the basic wings. The fouled anchor is 7/8 inch long. The height and width of the shield is 1/2 inch. Although Marines no longer wear these wings, they were once worn by balloon pilots during World War I and the Quantico based Balloon Company during the 1920's.

Naval Aircrew Insignia - Bronze, gold-plated metal pin consisting of the basic wings with a circular center design and anchor with the block letters "AC" superimposed. The circle diameter is 3/4 inch; anchor height is 1/2 inch. The Naval Aircrew Insignia is awarded to naval aircrewmen who have completed a locally administered course of instruction and are assigned as flight aircrew members. Assignments include: Helicopter crewchiefs, airborne electronic countermeasures operators, airborne radio operators and VG jet aircraft flight engineers.

Combat Aircrew Insignia - Oxidized silver-colored, winged metal pin, with a gold-colored circular shield with a superimposed fouled anchor; the word "AIRCREW" in raised letters on a silver-colored background below the circular shield; above the shield is a silver-colored scroll; the insignia measures two inches from wing tip to wing tip; circle on the shield, 5/16 inch in diameter. Gold stars, up to a total of three, as merited, are mounted on the scroll, necessary holes being pierced to receive them. A silver star may be used in lieu of three gold stars. The Combat Aircrew Insignia is awarded to aircrewmen who have participated in aerial flight during combat, and those enlisted personnel who qualify for nontechnical aircrew positions and serve in such positions in aerial combat. The Marine must be a volunteer and a regularly assigned member of a flight crew onboard a Marine aircraft participating in combat operations. The Marine must also be a graduate of an established course of instruction and/or OJT qualifying him for a position in the flight crew of a Marine aircraft. Combat aircrewmen who have qualified to wear combat stars may wear the Combat Aircrew Insignia on a permanent basis. A maximum of three combat stars may be awarded for display on the Combat Aircrew Insignia. The criteria for earning individual combat stars are as follows:

    a. Engagement of an enemy aircraft.
    b. Engagement of an enemy vessel with bombs, rockets, torpedoes, guns or missiles.
    c. Participation in offensive or defensive operations against enemy fortified positions.

A Marine who is qualified to wear the Naval Aircrew Insignia and the Combat Aircrew Insignia has the option of wearing the one of his choice.

Basic Parachutist Insignia - Oxidized silver pin about 1-1/2 inches long and 3/4 inch high, consisting of an open parachute flanked on either side by wings curving up and inward so that the tips join the edge of the parachute canopy. The Basic Parachutist Insignia is an Army insignia, but is awarded to Marine officers and enlisted personnel who have successfully completed a CG MCCDC (WF11B) approved parachuting course (i.e.: the Army Jump School at Fort Benning, Georgia).

Navy /Marine Corps Parachute Insignia - Bronze, gold-plated metal pin consisting of the basic aviation wings with a gold-colored open parachute centered on the wings. The parachute is ½ inch wide at its widest part and 13/16 inch long from top to bottom. The Navy /Marine Corps Parachute Insignia is awarded to Marine officers and enlisted personnel who have completed a CG MCCDC (WF11B) approved parachuting course, and completed five <u>additional</u> parachute jumps. The additional jumps must include at least one combat equipment day jump and two combat equipment night jumps. The additional jumps must also employ two or more types of military aircraft.

Senior Explosive Ordnance Disposal (EOD) Insignia - The same as the Basic EOD insignia, but with a 7/32 inch star on the drop bomb. The Senior EOD Insignia is awarded to Marine personnel in accordance with MCO 3571.2 (Criteria for Basic, Senior, and Master EOD). The Marine must have served in an EOD position for at least 36 months cumulative service following the award of the Basic EOD Insignia.

Basic Explosive Ordnance Disposal (EOD) Insignia - Oxidized silver pin consisting of a 1-inch high shield with a conventional drop bomb, point down, and four lightning bolts, all in front of a laurel leaf wreath 1-3/4 inches wide. The Basic EOD Insignia is awarded to Marine officers and enlisted personnel in accordance with MCO 3571.2 (Criteria for Basic, Senior, and Master EOD). The Marine must have successfully completed the basic EOD course taught at the US Naval EOD School, Indian Head, Maryland and be assigned to a position for which the course is a prerequisite. The wreath of the insignia symbolizes the achievements and laurels gained by EOD personnel. The bomb design is copied from the design of the World War II Bomb Disposal Badge and its three fins represent the major areas of nuclear, conventional and chemical/biological interests. The lightening bolts symbolize the potential destructive power and the courage and professionalism of the EOD personnel. The shield represents the EOD mission to prevent a detonation and protect personnel and property.

Master Explosive Ordnance Disposal (EOD) Insignia - The same as the Senior EOD insignia with a star in a laurel wreath above the shield. The Master EOD Insignia is awarded to Marine personnel in accordance with MCO 3571.2 (Criteria for Basic, Senior, and Master EOD). The Marine must have been awarded the Senior EOD Insignia, have at least 60 months cumulative service in an EOD position, and have been recommended by his immediate commander.

SCUBA Diver Insignia - Oxidized silver pin approximately 1-1/16 inches high, one inch wide, consisting of wet suit headgear and face mask with breathing apparatus around the neck. The SCUBA Diver Insignia is awarded to Marine officers and enlisted personnel who have completed a CG MCCDC (WF11B) approved underwater diving course.

Not more than two Marine Corps approved breast insignia are worn on the left, and not more than one foreign pilot or other U.S. service pilot /navigator insignia is worn on the right at a time. Miniature insignia, one-half regular size, are worn on evening dress jackets.

Ranks and Grades

A resolution of the Continental Congress established the Continental Marines on 10 November 1775. This resolution also established the basic officer grades of colonel, lieutenant colonel, major, and "other officer" as was usual in the Continental Army. The "other officer" phrase probably meant captain and lieutenant. Because of manpower shortages, the rank of major became the highest rank held by the Continental Marines during the Revolution and Samuel Nicholas held that billet. During the Revolution the emphasis was on ship's detachments, so the enlisted rank structure was quite simple. The grades that evolved were sergeant, corporal, drummer or fifer and private.

Following the Revolution the Continental Marines were disbanded and it wasn't until the Act of 27 March 1794 that the Marines were again authorized. During this period the emphasis continued to be for Marines to serve aboard ship. The Act allowed for ship's detachment of one lieutenant, one sergeant, one corporal, one drummer, one fifer and twenty-one privates.

The Act of 11 July 1798 created the Navy Department, and The United States Marine Corps came into being. This established a commissioned grade structure that exists to this day the with the ranks of major, captain, and first and second lieutenant. The new law also provided for staff noncommissioned officers, including the rank of sergeant major, quartermaster sergeant and drum major. The Act of 22 April 1800 established the rank of lieutenant colonel for the Commandant and abolished the rank of major until it was reinstated in 1809.

The next significant change in the rank structure was the innovation of the brevet rank, which was adopted after the War of 1812. Brevet ranks were conferred on officers who distinguished themselves in combat or had served ten years in any one grade. Brevet commissions in the Marine Corps date from the Act of Congress dated 16 April 1814. Following the war, the Act of 3 March 1817 decreed that the Commandant hold the rank of lieutenant colonel. The Act of 30 June 1834 provided for one colonel commandant. Colonel remained the highest rank in the Corps through the Civil War even though Archibald Henderson, the fifth Commandant, held the rank of brigadier general by brevet.

In 1867, the Marine Corps obtained its first regular commissioned brigadier general, when law elevated Commandant Jacob Zeilin to that rank. (The post of Commandant was permanently raised to brigadier general by statue on 3 March 1899.)

In 1899, following the War with Spain, a law was past that established enlisted grades and the authorized strength. The Act provided for 5 sergeants major, 1 drum major, 20 quartermaster sergeants and 72 billets for gunnery sergeants. This same law eliminated the rank of fifer in favor of the term "trumpeter," even though fifes were abandoned in 1881. 1899 also saw the leader of the Marine Band elevated from drum major to first lieutenant and the posts of adjutant and inspector, quartermaster and paymaster raised to the rank of colonel.

The Act of 21 May 1908 raised the prestige of the Corps by elevating the rank of the Commandant to major general. That same year the Marine Corps saw the need to reward Marines with technical skills by increasing pay without increasing rank. The additional pay was ear-marked for mess personnel, gun pointers, signalmen and those who demonstrated proficiency with weapons.

Warrant officers in the Marine Corps were authorized by the Act of 29 August 1916. This decision allowed the Corps to enter World War I with 20 new marine gunners and 20 new quartermaster clerks. The warrant rank of pay clerk was added in 1918 and the grade of private first class was authorized.

In the 1920's, Congress established the commissioned warrant grades of chief marine gunner, chief quartermaster and chief pay clerk. These commissioned ranks required six years of service and examination for promotion. During World War II, Congress abolished these ranks and established the grades of commissioned warrant officer and warrant officer.

During World War II, Congress created the title "Commandant of the Marine Corps" and raised the rank of the office twice to the rank of lieutenant general.

By the eve of World War II, the titles and pay grades of noncommissioned officers were varied, repetitive and complicated. Confusing titles like master technical sergeant first pay grade and mess sergeant, chief cook fourth grade brought about a need for readjustment. The first readjustments of enlisted rank structure started in 1941 and continued until 1 December 1946, when new rank designations went into effect. Branch titles were eliminated and the "square" or staff chevron was replaced with the "rocker" type chevron for all staff noncommissioned officers (see page 23). Between 1946 and 1958, there were only three significant changes in the enlisted rank structure. First, the Career Compensation Act of 12 October 1949 reversed the numbering of pay grades. Second, the addition of two new titles within the E-7 grade, and third, the Career Compensation Act of 1949 authorized two new pay grades, E-8 and E-9. On 25 November 1958 (effective 1 January 1959), the current rank structure went into effect, which is described on pages 22 and 23.

On 4 April 1945, Alexander A. Vandegrift was promoted to general and the Act of 7 August 1947 permanently raised the office of Commandant to the rank of general. The office of the Assistant Commandant was elevated to general on 2 June 1969.

In 1949, the pay grades W-4, W-3 and W-2 were established as commissioned warrant officers, and W-1 was established as warrant officer. In 1954, the title "chief warrant officer" replaced that of "commissioned warrant officer for those in the W-4, W-3, and W-2 pay grades (the 1990's saw the addition of the W-5 pay grade). In 1956, the title "marine gunner" was restored for qualified personnel appointed as nontechnical warrant officers. The title "marine gunner" has been discontinued several times since 1956, but it is currently in use to lend deserved prestige to the old line fighting Marine.

The terms, ranks and grades have been used interchangeably in this book. The Marine Corps has also used these terms interchangeably over the years. Evidence of this practice can be found in both Marine Corps Orders and correspondence. It should be noted, however, that the Marine Corps Manual now uses grades and/or grade structure exclusively with reference to rank only as it relates to rank in precedence.

Officer Rank Insignia

The Marine Corps officers' grade structure follows the other U.S. military services and uses the same rank structure as the Army and the Air Force. It should be noted that the rank insignia, although similar in appearance to the other services, has its own unique peculiarities (e.g.: the captain's and lieutenant's bars do not have a beveled edge, etc.)

The Officer grades in order of seniority are:

Rank	Pay Grade
General	O-10
Lieutenant General	O-9
Major General	O-8
Brigadier General	O-7
Colonel	O-6
Lieutenant Colonel	O-5
Major	O-4
Captain	O-3
First Lieutenant	O-2
Second Lieutenant	O-1
Chief Warrant Officer, CWO5	W-5
Chief Warrant Officer, CWO4	W-4
Chief Warrant Officer, CWO3	W-3
Chief Warrant Officer, CWO2	W-2
Warrant Officer, WO1	W-1
Marine Gunner	W-5 thru W-1

Officer rank insignia are worn on both epaulets of dress and service coats, as well as both collars of shirts and field and utility coats.

General Rank Insignia- Four silver-colored, five-pointed, stars. Shoulder stars are one inch in diameter and are either fastened together on a metal holding bar or placed individually with one point of each star in the same line; distance between the centers of adjacent stars is 3/4 inch. Collar stars are 9/16 inch in diameter and are fastened together on a metal holding bar in a straight line with one ray of each star pointing upward and at right angles to the holding bar.

Lieutenant General Rank Insignia - Three silver-colored stars, of the same type and arranged in the same manner as for a general, except the distance between centers of adjacent shoulder stars is one inch.

Major General Rank Insignia - Two silver-colored stars of the same type and arranged in the same manner as for a lieutenant general.

Brigadier General Rank Insignia - One silver-colored star.

Colonel Rank Insignia - A silver-colored spread eagle, right and left talons of one foot grasping an olive branch, the other, a bundle of arrows. Shoulder insignia; slightly curved, with 1-1/2-inch wing span. Collar insignia; flat, with 3-1/32 inch wing span.

Lieutenant Colonel Rank Insignia - A seven-pointed, silver-colored oak leaf, raised and veined. Shoulder insignia; slightly curved, one inch from stem tip to center leaf tip. Collar insignia: flat, 23/32 inch from stem tip to center leaf tip.

Major Rank Insignia - A seven-pointed, gold-colored oak leaf, raised and veined. Shoulder insignia; slightly curved, one inch from stem tip to center leaf tip. Collar insignia: flat, 23/32 inch from stem tip to center leaf tip.

Captain Rank Insignia - Two smooth silver-colored bars, without bevel, attached at each end by a holding bar. Shoulder insignia: each bar slightly curved, 1-1/8 inches long by 3/8 inch wide, and 3/8 inch apart. Collar insignia; flat, each bar 3/4 inch long by 1/4 inch wide and 1/4 inch apart.

First Lieutenant Rank Insignia - One silver-colored bar of the same type as for a captain.

Second Lieutenant Rank Insignia - One gold-colored bar of the same type as for a first lieutenant.

Chief Warrant Officer, CWO5 Rank Insignia - One silver-colored bar of the same type as for a first lieutenant with one scarlet enamel stripe superimposed lengthwise. Shoulder insignia; center enamel stripe is 1/8 inch wide and 1-1/8 inch long. Collar insignia; center enamel stripe is 1/8 inch wide and 3/4 inch long.

Chief Warrant Officer, CWO4 Rank Insignia - One silver-colored bar of the same type as for a first lieutenant with three scarlet enamel blocks superimposed. Shoulder insignia; center enamel block is 1/4 inch wide, with 1/8 inch wide outer blocks, 1/4 inch from the edges of the center block. Collar insignia; center enamel block is 5/32 inch wide, with 3/32 inch wide outer blocks, 5/32 inch from the edges of the center block.

Chief Warrant Officer, CWO3 Rank Insignia - One silver-colored bar of the same type as for a CWO-4 with two scarlet enamel blocks superimposed. Shoulder insignia blocks are 3/8 inch wide and 1/4 inch apart. Collar insignia; blocks are 1/4 inch wide and 5/32 inch apart.

Chief Warrant Officer, CWO2 Rank Insignia - One gold-colored bar of the same type as for a second lieutenant with three scarlet enamel blocks arranged in the same manner as for a CWO-4.

Warrant Officer, WO1 Rank Insignia - One gold-colored bar of the same type as for a CWO-2 with two scarlet enamel blocks arranged in the same manner as for a CWO-3.

Marine Gunner Insignia - One gold-colored replica of a bursting bomb (dress), one non-glossy black replica of a bursting bomb (service). Shoulder insignia; overall height of the bomb is about 1-1/4 inches. Collar insignia; flat, overall height of about 3/4 inch.

Evening Dress
Sleeve Ornamentation

Male Officers Female Officers

General Officers

Field Officers

Company Officers

Enlisted Rank and Service Insignia

The current Marine Corps enlisted grades in seniority are:

Rank	Pay Grade
Sergeant Major of the Marine Corps	E-9
Sergeant Major (Master Gunnery Sergeant)	E-9
First Sergeant (Master Sergeant)	E-8
Gunnery Sergeant	E-7
Staff Sergeant	E-6
Sergeant	E-5
Corporal	E-4
Lance Corporal	E-3
Private First Class	E-2
Private	E-1

Lance Corporal

Master Sergeant

First Sergeant

Sergeant Major

Master Gunnery Sergeant

The Marine Corps currently uses four types of rank insignia (chevrons): gold on red for the dress blue uniform (blues), green on red for the service uniform (greens), green on khaki for the service shirt and black metal on utilities (Women Marines wore green on white chevrons between 1952 and 1979 on the old green and white summer service uniform).

Staff Sergeant (Sleeve)   **Staff Sergeant (Collar)**

Enlisted rank insignia are worn on both sleeves of dress and service coats, jackets, and shirts as well as both collars of field and utility coats.

There have been a number of changes in the enlisted rank structure and rank insignia since the beginning of World War II (see page 23). During World War II the "line" staff non commissioned officers (those having command billets, dealing with command and personnel) had rounded "rockers" or "arcs" joined by chevrons, while staff staff non commissioned officers (those with technical skills in their field/MOS) had "ties" or straight bars joined by chevrons. These ties were abolished in December 1946 when it was decided that all staff noncommissioned officers would wear the rocker type chevron.

Platoon Sergeant   **Staff Sergeant**

During the Korean War period the Corps used chevrons and rockers and it was common practice during this period to stencil rank insignia on the sleeves of utilities jackets. The practice of using black metal collar rank insignia was also adopted after the Korean War and has been used on utilities collars since.

Sergeant   **Gunnery Sergeant**

In 1959, a new rank structure was approved which brought back the old Lance Corporal rank, added crossed rifles to the enlisted rank insignia and differentiated rank insignia between command and technical responsibilities at the E-8 and E-9, pay grades. The Lance Corporal rank replaced the old E-3 Corporal and "lifted" the balance of the rank structure as shown on page 23. The earlier addition of the E-8 and E-9, pay grades allowed senior Staff NCO's rank insignia to show those with command and personnel responsibilities as First Sergeant and Sergeant Major with a diamond and star respectively, and those with technical responsibilities as Master Sergeant and Master Gunnery Sergeant with crossed rifles and a bursting bomb.

Staff non commissioned Officers currently wear an 1890's style insignia on SNCO's evening dress jacket. This insignia is gold on scarlet.

Staff Sergeant   **Sgt Major of the Marine Corps**

Musicians in the Marine Band (The President's Own) currently wear rank insignia (E-6 to E-9) similar to their regular counterparts, except that the insignia contains a musical lyre rather than crossed rifles.

Marine Band Drum Major   **Marine Band Musician**

Enlistment, or service stripes, are worn on dress and service jackets, one for each four years of service. Service stripes are gold on red for the dress blue uniform (blues), green on red for the service uniform (greens). During the late 1950's and early 1960's service stripes were available green on khaki for the old Summer Service Coats (khaki), which was an optional uniform for Staff NCO's.

12 Years Service   **4 Years Service**

Enlisted Rank Structure

1944-1946		PAY GRADE	1946-1959		1959-PRESENT	
RANK	**INSIGNIA**		**RANK**	**INSIGNIA**	**RANK**	**INSIGNIA**
		E9	SGTMAJOR		1. SGTMAJOR* 2. MGYSGT	
		E8	1stSGT		1. 1stSGT 2. MSGT	
1. SGTMAJOR 1st SGT 2. MGYSGT MTSGT QMSGT PMSGT		E7	MSGT		GYSGT	
1. GYSGT 2. TECHSGT		E6	GYSGT		SSGT	
1. PLTSGT 2. SSGT		E5	SSGT		SGT	
SGT		E4	SGT		CPL	
CPL		E3	CPL		LANCE CPL	
PFC		E2	PFC		PFC	
PVT		E1	PVT		PVT	

Sergeant Major of the Marine Corps rank insignia includes the Marine Corps emblem flanked by stars.

Service/Identification Badges

The Presidential Service Badge (PSB), Vice Presidential Service Badge (VPSB), Office of the Secretary of Defense Identification Badge (OSD ID Badge), and Joint Chiefs of Staff Identification Badge (JCS ID Badge) are authorized to be worn on Marine Corps uniforms and can be worn after detachment from qualifying duty.

Presidential Service Badge (PSB)

The Presidential Service Badge was established on 1 September 1964. It replaced the White House Service Badge, which had been established on 1 June 1960. The badge is given by the President to members of the Armed Forces assigned to duty in the White House or to military units and support facilities under the administration of the Military Assistant to the President for a period of at least one year, after 20 January 1961, as recognition, in a permanent way, of their contribution in the service of the President. Once earned, the badge becomes a permanent part of the recipient's uniform and may be worn after the recipient leaves presidential service. The PSB consists of a blue enameled disc, 1-15/16 inches in diameter, surrounded by 27 gold rays radiating from the center. Superimposed on the disc is a gold-colored device taken from the seal of the President of the United States, encircled with 50 stars.

Vice Presidential Service Badge (VPSB) **(old)**

Vice Presidential Service Badge (VPSB) **(new)**

Vice Presidential Service Badge (VPSB)

The Vice Presidential Service Badge was established on 8 July 1970. The badge is awarded in the name of the Vice President to members of the Armed Forces who have been assigned to duty in the Office of the Vice President for a period of at least one-year after 20 January 1969. The first VPSB was 1-15/16 inches overall with a white enameled disc and satin gold rays along its edge. In the center was a gold eagle with drooping wings surrounded by 50 gold stars. The current VPSB consists of a white enameled disc, 1-15/16 inches in diameter surrounded by 27 gold rays radiating from the center. Superimposed on the disc is a gold-colored device taken from the seal of the Vice President of the United States. Once earned, the badge becomes a permanent part of the uniform.

Office of the Secretary of Defense Identification Badge (OSD ID)

The Office of the Secretary of Defense Identification Badge is worn by personnel who are assigned on a permanent basis to the following organizational elements:

1. Office of the Secretary and Deputy Secretary of Defense.
2. Offices of the Under Secretaries of Defense.
3. Offices of the Assistant Secretaries of Defense.
4. Office of the General Counsel of the Department of Defense.
5. Offices of the Assistants to the Secretary of Defense.
6. Office of the Defense Advisor, US Mission to the North Atlantic Treaty Organization (NATO).

After completion of one year of duty, the individual is entitled to permanent possession of the badge. A member of the Reserve Components who is assigned an authorized Reserve Forces position in OSD for a period of no less than two years, on or after 1 January 1973, is entitled to permanent possession of the badge. The OSD ID badge consists of an eagle with wings displayed horizontally, grasping three crossed gold arrows, and having on its breast an enameled shield consisting of a blue upper portion and 13 alternating red and white stripes on the lower portion; a gold ring passing behind the wing tips bearing 13 gold stars above the eagle and a wreath of laurel and olive in green enamel below the eagle; all superimposed on a silver sunburst of 33 rays two inches in diameter.

Full Size

Miniature

Joint Chiefs of Staff Identification Badge (JCS ID)

The Joint Chiefs of Staff Identification Badge is awarded to military personnel who have been assigned to duty and served not less than one year after 13 January 1961, in a position of responsibility under the direct cognizance of the Joint Chiefs of Staff. The award of the badge must be approved by the Chairman, Joint Chiefs of Staff; the head of a Directorate of the Joint Staff; or one of the subordinate agencies of the Organization of the Joint Chiefs of Staff. Personnel are authorized to wear the badge following reassignment from duty with the JCS. The standard size JCS ID badge consists of the United States shield (upper portion in blue, and 13 stripes of alternating red and white enamel) superimposed on four gold metal

unsheathed swords (two placed vertically and two diagonally), pointing to the top, with points and pommels resting on the wreath, blades and grips entwined with a gold metal continuous scroll surrounding the shield with the word "JOINT" at the top and the words "CHIEFS OF STAFF" at bottom, in blue enamel letters; all within an oval silver metal wreath of laurel 2-1/4 inches high by two inches wide.

Marines assigned to joint/unified commands may also be authorized to wear distinctive command identification badges, but only upon approval from the CMC (MCUB). Approved command identification devices are worn for the duration of assignment to that command only.

Marksmanship and Trophy Badges

The United States Marine Corps has historically encouraged and recognized proficiency with small arms and infantry weapons. Marksmanship has always been a priority with the Marine Corps, but serious marksmanship training and competition didn't begin until the early 1900's. The first levels of qualification were "Expert Rifleman," "Sharpshooter," and "Marksman." The first clear mention of these three marksmanship badges does not appear until 1912 in the Marine Corps Uniform Regulations. Mr. Kenneth L. Smith- Christmas, Curator of Material History of the Marine Corps Historical Center, believes, however, that marksmanship badges were aquired for issue to officers in the Corps as early as 1891.

Expert Rifleman Badge (Obsolete)

The first Marine Corps rifle marksmanship badges followed three basic designs in silver metal. The Expert Rifleman badge, for those who fired in the highest category of score, was a wreath on which two crossed M1903 Springfield rifles were superimposed and hung from a bar reading EXPERT RIFLEMAN.

Sharpshooter Badge (Obsolete)

The second category of qualification entitled the shooter to the Sharpshooter badge, which consisted of a four-branched Maltese cross with a three ringed target in the center suspended from a bar reading SHARPSHOOTER.

Rifle Marksman Badge (Obsolete)

The lowest qualification in marksmanship skill was the Marksman badge, which was a single bar reading MARKSMAN, bracketed by two small, ringed targets.

Requalification bars were commonly used during this period on both the Expert and Sharpshooter badges. These badges were used until 1924, when the Marine Corps adopted the bronze Army Expert, Sharpshooter and Marksman badges.

  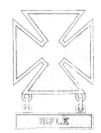

Army Expert Basic Qualification Badge *Army Sharpshooter Basic Qualification Badge* *Army Marksman, Basic Qualification Badge*

The Army marksmanship badges were used until 1937, when the Marine Corps returned to silver badges unique to the Corps. In 1937 the Marine Corps also adopted a newly designed "Basic badge," which survived until 1968 when it was declared obsolete. The Basic badge was awarded to Marines who had shown skill as experts and sharpshooters with the pistol and special weapons. The design of the Basic badge was similar to the old Expert Rifleman badge, which consisted of a wreath, centered under a three ring target, with a Marine Corps emblem at the top. This medallion was suspended from a bar reading U.S. MARINE CORPS. Qualification bars, sometimes called "Q"-bars, had the level of qualification ("EX" and "SS") preceding the weapon name and were suspended between the upper bar and the wreath.

Basic Badge with Expert Pistol Bar (Obsolete)

In July of 1958, the Marine Corps adopted the current series of marksmanship badges. The regulations called for three awards for both rifle and pistol with the addition of new requalification bars for both rifle and pistol.

Rifle Expert Badge

Wording changed from EXPERT RIFLEMAN to RIFLE EXPERT and Crossed M-1 rifles replaced the M1903 rifles on the Expert badge.

Rifle Sharpshooter Badge

The Sharpshooter badge was modified also, with a new bar with the word RIFLE SHARP-SHOOTER, and the target in the center of the Maltese cross was eliminated in favor of the Marine Corps emblem.

Rifle Marksman Badge

A square three ring target suspended from a bar with the words RIFLE MARKSMAN replaced the old Marksman badge.

Pistol Expert Badge

The Pistol Expert badge is similar to the Rifle Expert badge having a wreath on which two crossed M1911A1 pistols are superimposed. The Pistol Sharpshooter and Marksman badges are simply smaller versions of their rifle award counterparts and read "pistol" rather than "rifle."

Pistol Sharpshooter Badge   *Pistol Marksman Badge*

The Marine Corps has recently changed the long-familiar "Known Distance" rifle qualification course. New silhouette targets have replaced the old circular ringed "Able" targets and a new scoring system awards on a "hit or miss" system, rather than awarding points on proximity to the bull's eye. New positions now require Marines to shoot more rounds in the kneeling position and less in the sitting position. The new course is intended to focus qualification shooting away from competitive-style marksmanship toward the more practical aim of killing the enemy in combat.

During the course of this century, badges and qualification rules have changed, but the excellence in marksmanship still remains a major emphasis in the Corps.

Listed and illustrated as follows in order of precedence, are the marksmanship awards authorized for wear on the Marine Corps uniform.

1. U.S. Distinguished International Shooter Badge (Gold)

2. Distinguished Marksman Badge (Gold)

3. Distinguished Pistol Shot Badge (Gold)

4. Lauchheimer Trophy Badge (Gold)
5. Lauchheimer Trophy Badge (Silver)
6. Lauchheimer Trophy Badge (Bronze)

7. McDougle Trophy Badge (Gold) Marine Corps Rifle Championship Badge

8. Walsh Trophy Badge (Gold) Marine Corps Pistol Championship Badge

9. Marine Cops Rifle Competition Badge (Gold) National Trophy Rifle Match Badge (Gold) Interservice Rifle Match Badge (Gold)

10. Marine Corps Pistol Competition Badge (Gold) National Trophy Pistol Match Badge (Gold) Interservice Pistol Match Badge (Gold)

11. Marine Corps Rifle Competition Badge (Silver) National Trophy Rifle Match Badge (Silver) Interservice Rifle Match Badge (Silver)

12. Marine Corps Pistol Competition Badge (Silver) National Trophy Pistol Match Badge (Silver) Interservice Pistol Match Badge (Silver)

13. Marine Corps Rifle Competition Badge (Bronze) National Trophy Rifle Match Badge (Bronze) Interservice Rifle Match Badge (Bronze)

14. Marine Corps Pistol Competition Badge (Bronze) National Trophy Pistol Match Badge (Bronze) Interservice Pistol Match Badge (Bronze)

15. Inter-Division Rifle Competition Badge (Gold)

16. Inter-Division Pistol Competition Badge (Gold)

17. FMF Combat Infantry Trophy Match Badge (Bronze)

18. Annual Rifle Squad Combat Practice Competition Badge (Gold)

19. Annual Rifle Squad Combat Practice Competition Badge (Silver)

20. Annual Rifle Squad Combat Practice Competition Badge (Bronze)

21. Division Rifle Competition Badge (Gold)National Board for the Promotion of Rifle Practice Rifle Badge (Gold)

22. Division Pistol Competition Badge (Gold) National Board for the Promotion of Pistol Practice Rifle Badge (Gold)

23. Division Rifle Competition Badge (Silver) National Board for the Promotion of Rifle Practice Rifle Badge (Silver)

24. Division Pistol Competition Badge (Silver) National Board for the Promotion of Pistol Practice Rifle Badge (Silver)

25. Division Rifle Competition Badge (Bronze) National Board for the Promotion of Rifle Practice Rifle Badge (Bronze)

26. Division Pistol Competition Badge (Bronze) National Board for the Promotion of Pistol Practice Rifle Badge (Bronze)

27. San Diego, Wharton, Elliott, Wirgman, Lloyd, and Smith Trophy Rifle Team Match Badges (Gold)

28. Holcomb, Edson, Shively, and Finn (Pacific) Trophy Pistol Team Match Badges (Gold)

29. Rifle Qualification Badges
    a. Expert (with last qualification bar)
    b. Sharpshooter
    c. Marksman

30. Pistol Qualification Badges
    a. Expert (with last qualification bar)
    b. Sharpshooter
    c. Marksman

Aiguillettes, Breastcords, Shoulder Cords and Fourragere

Aiguillettes - Aides de Camp

Aiguillettes are worn by Marine officers to identify them as aides to top-ranking government officials and general officers. Aiguillettes are worn with both service and dress uniforms. Aiguillettes are worn on the right shoulder by aides to the President, Vice-President, foreign heads of state, and White House aides. All others wear the aiguillettes on the left shoulder

Service Aiguillettes

Service aiguillettes are of round gold wire and scarlet cord, 1/4 inch in diameter, and consist of two, three, or four loops sewn together all the way around. The lengths of the cords forming loops are: The first/inside loop, 27 inches; the second loop, 28-1/2 inches; third loop, 28-3/8 inches, and fourth loop, 30-3/4 inches. Where the ends meet, the cords are fitted with a bar pin about 1-1/2 inches long by 3/8 inch wide and bound together with a 1-1/2 inch strip of No. 3 gold braid covering the ends of the cord to allow attachment of the aiguillettes to uniform coats at the shoulder, just inside the armhole seam. Service aiguillettes consist of loops which indicate:

Four Loops - Personal aides to the President or Vice President; aides at the White House; aides to the Secretary or Deputy Secretary of Defense, Secretary or Under Secretary of the Navy, and Assistant Secretaries of Defense or the Navy; aide to the General Counsel of the Navy; and naval attaches and assistant attaches assigned to an embassy.

Four Loops - Aides to generals, admirals, or officials of higher grade.

Three Loops - Aides to lieutenant generals and vice admirals.

Two Loops - Aides to major/brigadier generals, rear admirals, or other officers of lower grade entitled to an aide.

Two Loops - Officers appointed as aides to a governor of a state or territory may wear aiguillettes on official occasions.

Dress Aiguillettes

Dress aiguillettes are of round gold cord 1/4 inch in diameter, with a core of yellow cotton covered with gold or gilt thread. They consist of two cords made in three plaits, with a pencil attachment on the end of each plaited cord, and of two loops of single cord. The rear-plaited cord is 28 inches long and the front-plaited cord is 20 inches long; the front single cord is 17 inches long and the rear single cord is 21 inches long. The two-plaited cords and front single loop (after the latter has been passed through rear single loop) are securely fastened together and have a 1-inch loop of No. 9 gold braid for attaching aiguillettes to top button of coat, collar opening of dress coat, or button or hook of jackets; the rear plaited cord passing over the front plaited cord and fastening underneath the front plaited cord at the loop. From the point where the cords are secured together, the two plaited cords extend as single cords for two inches, then they form coils of five laps, ends passing through coils and extending two inches to gilt pencil attachment. The position separating the front and rear plaited cords is fitted with a bar pin about 1-1/2 inches long and 3/8 inch wide, covered with a 1-1/2 inch strip of No. 3 gold braid covering the ends of the cord, and the bar, to allow attaching the aiguillette to the coat or jacket at the shoulder, just inside the armhole seam. The pencil attachment is gold-plated brass, 3.015 inches long, the cap is 0.656 inches long, and the pencil is 2.359 inches long. The cap has six leaves; the pencil has two miniature Marine Corps emblems (omitting motto ribbon and anchor rope) on the upper part and two wreaths on the lower part, all in relief around the circumference. The smooth surfaces are polished; the cap or upper part is stamped; and the lower part hollow-cast, turned, milled, and knurled.

Dress aiguillettes are the same regardless of the rank of the individual being served.

Musician - Marine Band (President's Own)
(Marine Corps Art Collection)

Bugler - Marine Drum & Bugle Corps (Commandant's Own)
(Marine Corps Art Collection)

Aiguillettes - Marine Band

Aiguillettes are also worn on the full dress uniforms by members of the Marine Band. Gold plaited aiguillettes are worn by officers, while enlisted members wear white braid aiguillettes. These aiguillettes are worn from the left shoulder knot with cords worn in front of the arm and the loop suspended from the center top button of the coat.

Breastcords - Marine Drum & Bugle Corps

Scarlet and gold breastcords are worn on the dress and service uniforms by members of the Marine Drum & Bugle Corps. These cords are worn when prescribed by the commander, but not on the utility uniform. The cords are worn from the left shoulder. Scarlet and gold breastcords are also worn on the dress uniforms by enlisted Marines on duty at the White House. The cords are worn from the left shoulder.

Shoulder Cords

Fourragere

Blue Dress Coat

Shoulder Cords - Female Drill Instructors

Shoulder cords were worn by female drill instructors at MCRD, Parris Island from November 1984 until October 1996, replacing cloth epaulets worn from 1969 to 1984. The cords were scarlet and worn on the left shoulder of both service and utility uniform. These cords were referred by many DI's as "the big Irish pennant," in October 1996, the cords were retired when female drill instructors were authorized to wear the same field hat (campaign cover) worn by male drill instructors.

Fourragere

The fourragere was awarded by the French Ministry of War, during World War I, to units which were cited two or more times in the French Orders of the Army. The 5th and 6th Marines were so cited and all personnel are authorized to wear the fourragere while serving in these units. The fourragere is dark green and red, the colors of the ribbon of the Croix de Guerre. The fourragere is worn over the left shoulder with the left arm passing through the large loop of the cord; the small loop will engage the button under the shoulder strap. The metal pencil attachment will hang naturally to the front.

Shoulder Patches

The Marine Corps authorized the wearing of shoulder patches, properly called shoulder insignia, first during World War I and then again in March 1943, when LOI No. 372 authorized insignia for the 1st, 2nd, and 3rd Divisions, aircraft wings, and certain other specified units. They were worn on the left sleeve of service coats and overcoats. During the latter part of World War II nearly every Marine wore a shoulder patch identifying his unit. Initially these patches were referred to as "battle blazes" and were intended to commemorate battles fought by the unit; the 1st Division designed their shoulder patch with the title "Guadalcanal". Most of these patches identified the number associated with the unit, but the 1st Division was the only unit to include the name of an actual battle in the design.

These distinctive designs were not only used as uniform shoulder patches, but were also used during World War II on signs, letter heads, and shooting jacket emblems, etc. This practice was short-lived after the war however, since the practice of wearing shoulder patches on uniforms was abolished on 23 September 1947 (effective 1 January 1948). These uniform shoulder insignia were abolished on the grounds that the Marine Corps is a unified body organized to fight as a whole and individual shoulder patches did not reflect the spirit of the Corps.

During the Korean Conflict these designs unofficially reappeared as unit signs, but not on uniforms. In 1956 Headquarters Marine Corps re-thought the policy and approved the use of organizational distinguishing marks on everything but uniforms (the exception being G-1 flight jackets and flight suits). Because of this change in policy the practice of using patches accelerated during the Viet Nam era and is alive and well today. Many of these patches and others referred to as "novelty patches" were derived from those used in World War II and are too numerous for reproduction in this publication. Pages 54 and 55 show many, but certainly not all, of the shoulder patches worn during World War II and early post war period.

1st Marine Division

The "Guadalcanal Blaze" of the 1st Marine Division was the first Divisional Patch created during World War II and was designed by Lt. Col. M.B. Twining who served as the G-3 (Operations) during the Guadalcanal campaign. The badge shows the numeral one inscribed with the name "Guadalcanal" on a blue background.

2nd Marine Division (early version)   *2nd Marine Division*

The patch of the 2nd Marine Division was at first on a blue background like the 1st Division and depicted a snake in the form of numeral two with the Guadalcanal battle honor. This was later changed to a hand holding a torch and the Southern Cross on a red/scarlet arrowhead background.

3rd Marine Division   *4th Marine Division*

5th Marine Division   *6th Marine Division*

The patch of the 3rd Marine Division became a three-pointed star or "caltrop" on a red curvilinear triangle. A figure "4" on a red diamond became the 4th Marine Division insignia. The 5th Marine Division chose a red shield with a "V" (for victory and the Roman numeral). The 6th Marine Division Patch was a blue circle with the numeral "6" and the three area designations: "Melanesia," "Micronesia" and "Orient."

Pacific Air Wings Headquarters   *1st Marine Air Wing*

The approved Air Wing insignia design was "kite-shaped," red/scarlet with yellow/gold wings extending from a Marine Corps emblem above the black letters PAC for Pacific Air Wing Headquarters and black Roman numerals indicating each wing.

FMF Pacific Artillery Bn.   *FMF Pacific Anti-Aircraft Artillery*   *FMF Pacific Bomb Disposal Co.*   *Marine Ships' Detachments Afloat*   *Aircraft Fuselage 4th Wing*   *1st Marine Brigade (Iceland)*

The Fleet Marine Force, Pacific (FMFPAC) personnel wore an insignia in the form of a red/scarlet shield with an eagle at the top, whose outstretched wings form the top of the shield. Below the wings were the words, "FMF-PAC" and the three stars of a lieutenant general. In the center of the insignia is a gold circle where the various unit designations (Artillery, Anti-Aircraft Artillery, Bomb Disposal, etc.) can be found.

Marine patches typically used red/scarlet as a background color and usually bore the number of the organization, symbolic defense weapons, or other symbols such as the alligator, dragon, or sea horse in the insignia in yellow/gold. The reason for this color scheme was Marine Corps Order No. 4 (dtd. 18 April 1925), which designated scarlet and gold as the official colors of the Corps.

1st MAC Defense Bn.   *1st MAC Aviation Engineers*   *1st MAC Raiders*

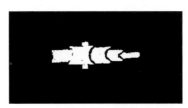

Gun Captain   *Gun Pointer 2nd Class*

The First Marine Amphibious Corps (1MAC) was established on 1 October 1942 and coordinated the first American offensive of World War II. The shoulder insignia of the Marine Amphibious Corps was a blue shield with the stars of the Southern Cross constellation and a red diamond in the center. Units of 1MAC consisted of Artillery, Aviation Engineers, a Barrage Balloon Battalion, a Defense Battalion, a Parachute Battalion, four Marine Raider Battalions and a Service Supply Battalion. Symbols denoting these various organizations were placed inside the red diamond of the insignia.

Gun Pointer 1st Class

3rd Amphibious Corps   *5th Amphibious Corps*   *13th Marine Defense Bn.*

Parachute Man   *Gunnery "E"*

The Third and Fifth Amphibious Corps were established later in World War II and each used a red/scarlet shield as an insignia. The IIIAC used a yellow/gold Chinese dragon and a Roman numeral "III", while the VAC used the head of a yellow/gold alligator and the three white stars of its commander, Lieutenant General Holland M. "Howling Mad" Smith.

During World War II, Marines serving in ships' detachments, were authorized to wear cloth insignia on their lower left sleeve indicating Gun Captain, Gun Pointer - 1st Class, Gun Pointer - 2nd Class, Parachute Man and an excellence in Gunnery "E" device. These Navy style distinguishing marks were white on navy for blues and red on forest green on greens.

Awards and Decorations

The United States Marine Corps, being part of the U.S. Naval Service, follows the same awards program as the United States Navy. The awards program is governed by the Department of the Navy, but administered by the Corps. Most of the awards and decorations are the same for both the Navy and Marine Corps and some are common to all services.

Marine Corps awards fall into three classifications: personal and unit decorations, campaign and service medals, and marksmanship badges and trophies.

Personal awards are conferred upon individuals for acts of heroism, acts of gallantry, or for meritorious service.

Unit decorations are awarded to individuals who are members of units that are cited for outstanding performance.

Campaign or service medals are issued to individuals who participate in particular campaigns or periods of service for which a medal is authorized.

Marksmanship badges and trophies are awarded to individuals who demonstrate a proficiency or skill with a specific weapon during a specified practice exercise, competition or match. Marksmanship badges are worn to indicate an individual's ability with a specific weapon and are awarded in three levels: Expert, Sharpshooter and Marksman. Trophies are awarded at various levels to include: United States and international distinguished shooter competitions, Marine Corps rifle and pistol championships, national trophies for rifle and pistol, inter-service rifle and pistol matches, regional practices, combat exercises, division and inter-division contests.

Badges are awarded to indicate proficiency in specific areas, such as marksmanship. The Marine Corps also participates with the other services in a system by which entire units are recognized for outstanding performance. Members of cited units are entitled to wear the appropriate award (e.g.: Navy Presidential Unit Citation and Navy Unit Commendation, etc.).

Marines may wear awards described in the Navy and Marine Corps Awards Manual (SECNAVINST 1650.1). The definition of terms according to Marine Corps Uniform Regulations are:

Award - An all-inclusive term covering any decoration, medal, badge, ribbon bar, or attachment bestowed on an individual.

Decoration - An award conferred on an individual for a specific act of gallantry or for meritorious service.

Unit Award - An award made to an operating unit for outstanding performance and worn only by members of that unit who participated in the cited action.

Service Award - An award made to those who have participated in designated wars, campaigns, expeditions, etc., or who have fulfilled specified service requirements.

Medal - An award issued to an individual for performance of certain duties, acts or services, consisting of a medallion hanging from a suspension ribbon of distinctive colors.

Miniature Medal - A replica of a standard size medal, made to one-half original scale. Foreign medal miniatures will not exceed the size of American miniatures. The Medal of Honor will not be worn in miniature.

Badge - An award to an individual for some special proficiency or skill, which consists of a medallion suspended from a bar or bars.

Ribbon Bar - A portion of the suspension ribbon of a medal, worn in lieu of the medal. Ribbon bars are also authorized for certain awards which have no medals.

Rosette - Lapel device made by gathering the suspension ribbon of the medal into a circular shape.

Lapel Pin - A miniature enameled replica of the ribbon bar.

Attachment - Any appurtenance such as a star, clasp, or other device worn on a suspension ribbon of a medal or on the ribbon bar (also called device).

Types of Medals, Ribbons and Attachments

There are two general categories of "medals" awarded by the United States to its military personnel, namely, decorations and service medals.

The terms "decoration" and "medal" are used almost interchangeably today (as they are in this book), but there are recognizable distinctions between them. Decorations, are awarded for acts of gallantry and meritorious service and usually have distinctive (and often unique) shapes such as crosses or stars (there are exceptions to this, such as the Navy DSM, which is round). Medals are awarded for good conduct, participation in a particular campaign or expedition, or a noncombatant service and normally come in a round shape. The fact that some very prestigious awards have the word "medal" in their titles (e.g.: <u>Medal</u> of Honor, Marine Corps Brevet <u>Medal</u>, Navy and Marine Corps <u>Medal</u>, etc.) can cause some confusion.

There are three different forms of medals (and decorations) for wear on the uniform: the full size medal, the miniature medal and the ribbon bar. The wearing of medals on the uniform is covered in the section "Wearing Medals, Ribbons, Badges and Insignia" starting on page 107.

The miniature medal, the enameled lapel button or pin and the civilian hatpin may be worn on civilian clothing, and are discussed on page 106.

Decoration   Service Medal

Small metal attachments or devices are worn on the medal suspension ribbon and ribbon bar to denote additional awards, campaigns or subsequent service. These attachments come in the form of ⭐ stars, 🌿 oak leaf clusters, 3 numerals, E letters, etc. The attachments and manner of placement are described in detail in the section "Attachments and Devices" starting on page 38.

Different Forms of Medals

Basic Ribbon Bar

Lapel Pin

Miniature Medal

Civilian Hatpin

Full Size Medal

Reverse of Medal

Ribbon Bar with Appropriate Attachments

U.S. Award Certificates

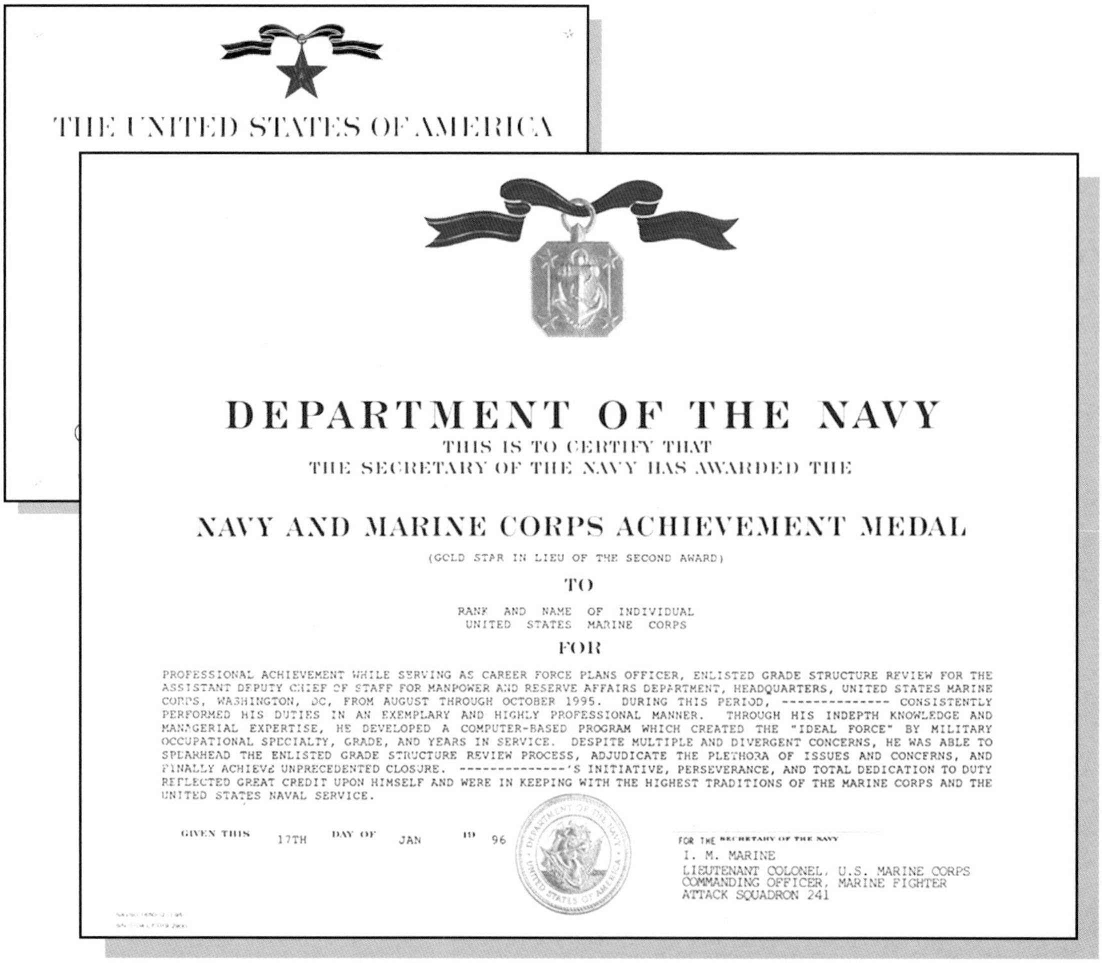

THE UNITED STATES OF AMERICA

DEPARTMENT OF THE NAVY
THIS IS TO CERTIFY THAT
THE SECRETARY OF THE NAVY HAS AWARDED THE

NAVY AND MARINE CORPS ACHIEVEMENT MEDAL
(GOLD STAR IN LIEU OF THE SECOND AWARD)

TO

RANK AND NAME OF INDIVIDUAL
UNITED STATES MARINE CORPS

FOR

PROFESSIONAL ACHIEVEMENT WHILE SERVING AS CAREER FORCE PLANS OFFICER, ENLISTED GRADE STRUCTURE REVIEW FOR THE
ASSISTANT DEPUTY CHIEF OF STAFF FOR MANPOWER AND RESERVE AFFAIRS DEPARTMENT, HEADQUARTERS, UNITED STATES MARINE
CORPS, WASHINGTON, DC, FROM AUGUST THROUGH OCTOBER 1995. DURING THIS PERIOD, -------------- CONSISTENTLY
PERFORMED HIS DUTIES IN AN EXEMPLARY AND HIGHLY PROFESSIONAL MANNER. THROUGH HIS INDEPTH KNOWLEDGE AND
MANAGERIAL EXPERTISE, HE DEVELOPED A COMPUTER-BASED PROGRAM WHICH CREATED THE "IDEAL FORCE" BY MILITARY
OCCUPATIONAL SPECIALTY, GRADE, AND YEARS IN SERVICE. DESPITE MULTIPLE AND DIVERGENT CONCERNS, HE WAS ABLE TO
SPEARHEAD THE ENLISTED GRADE STRUCTURE REVIEW PROCESS, ADJUDICATE THE PLETHORA OF ISSUES AND CONCERNS, AND
FINALLY ACHIEVE UNPRECEDENTED CLOSURE. --------------'S INITIATIVE, PERSEVERANCE, AND TOTAL DEDICATION TO DUTY
REFLECTED GREAT CREDIT UPON HIMSELF AND WERE IN KEEPING WITH THE HIGHEST TRADITIONS OF THE MARINE CORPS AND THE
UNITED STATES NAVAL SERVICE.

GIVEN THIS   17TH   DAY OF   JAN   19 96

FOR THE SECRETARY OF THE NAVY

I. M. MARINE
LIEUTENANT COLONEL, U.S. MARINE CORPS
COMMANDING OFFICER, MARINE FIGHTER
ATTACK SQUADRON 241

Current Department of the Navy Certificate

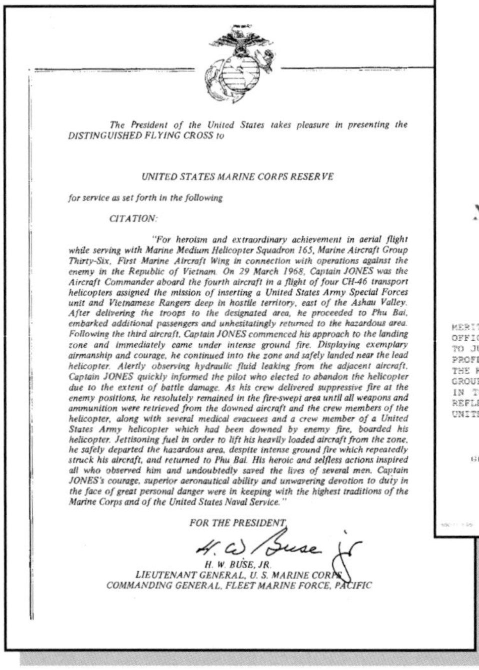

The President of the United States takes pleasure in presenting the
DISTINGUISHED FLYING CROSS to

UNITED STATES MARINE CORPS RESERVE

for service as set forth in the following

CITATION:

"For heroism and extraordinary achievement in aerial flight
while serving with Marine Medium Helicopter Squadron 165, Marine Aircraft Group
Thirty-Six, First Marine Aircraft Wing in connection with operations against the
enemy in the Republic of Vietnam. On 29 March 1968, Captain JONES was the
Aircraft Commander aboard the fourth aircraft in a flight of four CH-46 transport
helicopters assigned the mission of inserting a United States Army Special Forces
unit and Vietnamese Rangers deep in hostile territory, east of the Ashau Valley.
After delivering the troops to the designated area, he proceeded to Phu Bai,
embarked additional passengers and unhesitatingly returned to the hazardous area.
Following the third aircraft, Captain JONES commenced his approach to the landing
zone and immediately came under intense ground fire. Displaying exemplary
airmanship and courage, he continued into the zone and safely landed near the lead
helicopter. Alertly observing hydraulic fluid leaking from the adjacent aircraft,
Captain JONES quickly informed the pilot who elected to abandon the helicopter
due to the extent of battle damage. As his crew delivered suppressive fire at the
enemy positions, he resolutely remained in the fire-swept area until all weapons and
ammunition were retrieved from the downed aircraft and the crew members of the
helicopter, along with several medical evacuees and a crew member of a United
States Army helicopter which had been downed by enemy fire, boarded his
helicopter. Jettisoning fuel in order to lift his heavily loaded aircraft from the zone,
he safely departed the hazardous area, despite intense ground fire which repeatedly
struck his aircraft. and returned to Phu Bai. His heroic and selfless actions inspired
all who observed him and undoubtedly saved the lives of several men. Captain
JONES's courage, superior aeronautical ability and unwavering devotion to duty in
the face of great personal danger were in keeping with the highest traditions of the
Marine Corps and of the United States Naval Service."

FOR THE PRESIDENT,

H. W. BUSE, JR.
LIEUTENANT GENERAL, U. S. MARINE CORPS
COMMANDING GENERAL, FLEET MARINE FORCE, PACIFIC

DEPARTMENT OF THE NAVY
THIS IS TO CERTIFY THAT
THE SECRETARY OF THE NAVY HAS AWARDED THE

NAVY AND MARINE CORPS COMMENDATION MEDAL
(GOLD STAR IN LIEU OF THE SECOND AWARD)

TO
RANK AND NAME OF INDIVIDUAL
UNITED STATES MARINE CORPS

FOR

MERITORIOUS SERVICE WHILE SERVING CONSECUTIVELY AS ASSISTANT OFFICER IN CHARGE AND MECHANIZED SUPPLY TEAM
OFFICER, FIELD SUPPLY AND MAINTENANCE ANALYSIS OFFICE-3, MARINE CORPS BASE, CAMP BUTLER, JAPAN, FROM JUNE 1992
TO JUNE 1995. DURING THIS PERIOD, ----------- CONSISTENTLY PERFORMED HIS DUTIES IN AN EXEMPLARY AND HIGHLY
PROFESSIONAL MANNER. THROUGH HIS INDEPTH KNOWLEDGE AND RESOURCEFUL MANAGEMENT, HE WAS INSTRUMENTAL IN PROVIDING
THE RESOLUTION OF HISTORIC ACCOUNTABILITY AND PROPERTY CONTROL DYSFUNCTIONS WITHIN THE 3D FORCE SERVICE SUPPORT
GROUP TRAINING ALLOWANCE POOL, AS WELL AS THE IDENTIFICATION AND ARTICULATION OF CRITICAL SUPPLY SUPPORT ISSUES
IN THE AREA OF MEDICAL LOGISTICS. -----------'S INITIATIVE, PERSEVERANCE, AND TOTAL DEDICATION TO DUTY
REFLECTED GREAT CREDIT UPON HIMSELF AND WERE IN KEEPING WITH THE HIGHEST TRADITIONS OF THE MARINE CORPS AND THE
UNITED STATES NAVAL SERVICE.

GIVEN THIS   3D   DAY OF JAN   19 96

FOR THE SECRETARY OF THE NAVY

I. M. MARINE
LIEUTENANT GENERAL, U.S. MARINE CORPS
I MARINE EXPEDITIONARY FORCE

Vietnam Era Marine Award Certificate

Foreign Award Certificates

**Republic of Vietnam's Gallantry Cross Award
Certificate and Orders**

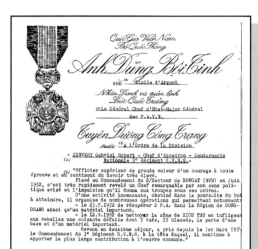

RVN Civil Award Certificate

**NATO Award Certificate for
Current NATO Medal**

**Saudi Arabian Award Certificate for
Liberation of Kuwait Medal**

Attachments and Devices

Stars, clasps, numerals, letter devices, and other devices are worn on the suspension ribbons of large and miniature medals, and on ribbon bars. Interestingly, each service has different regulations covering how they are worn. The wearing of attachments and devices, covered in this book, is taken from Marine Corps Uniform Regulations and is, in many cases, unique to the Marine Corps and the Naval Service. *(The terms, attachments and devices are used interchangeably in this book.)*

In the Marine Corps, stars are worn with one ray pointing up. On large and miniature medals, if one star is authorized, it will be centered on the suspension ribbon and if more than one star is authorized, the stars will be evenly spaced in a vertical line at the center of the suspension ribbon with the senior star at the top. On ribbon bars, if one star is authorized, it is centered, and if more than one star is authorized, the stars are evenly spaced in a horizontal line. Silver star(s) worn with bronze or gold star(s) are worn as previously mentioned, except that the first bronze star is placed to the wearer's left of the silver star(s) with additional stars alternating to the right of the silver star and so on.

 Gold Stars - A gold star is worn on suspension ribbons of large and miniature medals and ribbon bars for all personal decorations in lieu of a second or subsequent award.

 Silver Stars - A silver star is worn on suspension ribbons of large and miniature medals and ribbon bars in lieu of five gold stars, or in lieu of five bronze stars.

 Bronze Stars - A bronze star is worn on suspension ribbons of large and miniature medals and ribbon bars to indicate a second or subsequent award or to indicate major engagements in which an individual participated.

 Letter "V" - A bronze letter "V" is worn on specific combat decorations if the award is approved for valor (heroism). The specific combat decorations are; Distinguished Flying Cross, Bronze Star Medal, Air Medal, Joint Service Commendation Medal and the Navy and Marine Corps Commendation and Achievement Medals. Only one "V" is worn and gold, bronze, or silver stars, or oak leaf clusters are evenly spaced in a vertical line above the "V" on suspension ribbons of large and miniature medals. They are evenly spaced in a horizontal line on the ribbon bar with the "V" at the center.

 Letter "E" - A silver letter "E" is worn on the Navy "E" ribbon. Additional awards are denoted by additional "E"s. Four or more awards are denoted by an "E" surrounded by a silver wreath.

 Strike/Flight Numerals - Bronze strike/Flight numerals are worn on the Air Medal to indicate the total number of Strike/Flight awards received after 9 April, 1962. The Arabic numerals are placed symmetrically below the center of the suspension ribbons of large and miniature medals and to the wearer's left on the ribbon bar.

 Single Mission /Individual Numerals - Gold single Mission/Individual numerals were worn on the Air Medal to indicate the total number of Single Mission/Individual awards received (from 1980 to 1989). The Arabic numerals were placed symmetrically above the center of the suspension ribbons of large and miniature medals and to the wearers right on the ribbon bar. A bronze letter "V" (Combat Distinguishing Device), if authorized, was centered directly below the Single Mission/Individual numerals on suspension ribbons of large and miniature medals.

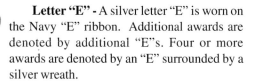

Navy Occupation Service Medal Clasp - The bronze Navy Occupation Service Medal clasp marked "EUROPE" and/or "ASIA" is worn on suspension ribbons of large and miniature Navy Occupation Service Medals to denote service in Europe and/or Asia.

 Atlantic Fleet "A" - The block letter "A" was authorized for wear on the ribbon bar and medal suspension ribbon of the American Defense Service Medal by personnel who served in the Atlantic Fleet on the high seas prior to the outbreak of World War II.

WINTERED OVER

Antarctica Service Medal Clasp - The bronze Antarctica Service Medal clasp marked "WINTERED OVER" is worn on the suspension ribbon of the large Antarctica Service Medal to denote service in the Antarctic Continent during the winter months. A gold clasp is worn to denote the second winter and a silver clasp for the third. Only one clasp is worn.

Oak Leaf Cluster - A bronze Oak Leaf Cluster denotes a second or subsequent award of a personal decoration or the Joint Service Awards bestowed upon a Marine by the Department of Defense. The Oak Leaf Cluster is a twig of four oak leaves and is worn on suspension ribbons of large and miniature medals and ribbon bars. The twig is worn with the stem of the oak leaves toward the wearer's right. A silver Oak Leaf Cluster is worn in lieu of five bronze Oak Leaf Clusters.

 Hour Glass - A bronze hour glass device denotes ten years service on the Armed Forces Reserve Medal. Upon the completion of the ten year period, reservists that are not mobilized are awarded the Armed Forces Reserve Medal with a bronze hourglass device. Silver and gold hourglass devices are awarded at the end of twenty and thirty years of reserve service, respectively. The device represents an hourglass with the Roman numeral X superimposed thereon. It is worn centered on the suspension ribbons of large and miniature medals and ribbon bars.

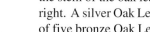 **Letter "M" -** A bronze letter "M" on the Armed Forces Reserve Medal denotes reservists mobilized and called to active duty.

 Antarctica Continental Disc - A bronze Antarctica Continental Disc is worn on the suspension ribbon of the miniature medal and ribbon bar of the Antarctica Service Medal. A bronze disc denotes wintering over. A gold and silver disc denotes a second and third winter.

 Vietnam "1960-" Device - The Vietnam "1960-" Device is worn by Marines authorized to wear the Republic of Vietnam Campaign Medal. The silver banner device with the numerals "1960-" is worn on the suspension ribbon of the large and miniature medals and ribbon bars.

 Letter "W" - A silver letter "W" denotes participation in Defense of Wake Island.

WAKE ISLAND

Frames - A gold frame is worn on ribbon bars for foreign unit awards. The frame is gold plated matte finish with polished highlights. The frame is worn so that the leaves at either end will form a "V."

 Airplane – The Berlin Airlift Device, a three-eighths inch gold C-54 airplane, is authorized to be worn on the ribbon bar and suspension ribbon of the Navy Occupation Service Medal by Naval and Marine Personnel who served 90 consecutive days in support of the Berlin Airlift (1948-1949).

 Palm - A bronze palm is attached to the ribbon bar of the of the Republic of Vietnam Gallantry Cross Unit Citation and the Republic of Vietnam Civil Actions Unit Citation denoting that the awards were awarded at the Armed Forces level.

 Crossed Swords and Palm Tree - The emblem of Saudi Arabia (crossed swords and a palm tree) is affixed to the center of the ribbon bar of the Kuwait Liberation Medal (Saudi Arabia).

(All attachments are shown oversized. See page 117 for placement)

Right Breast Ribbons When Wearing Medals (as seen from the front)

The Marine Corps prescribes the wear of "ribbon-only" awards on the <u>right</u> breast of the full dress uniform when large medals are worn. The required display is as follows:

(Marine Corps Art Collection)

Combat Action Ribbon	Navy Presidential Unit Citation	Joint Meritorious Unit Award
Navy Unit Commendation	Navy Meritorious Unit Commendation	Navy "E" Ribbon
Navy Sea Service Deployment Ribbon	Arctic Service Ribbon	Navy & Marine Corps Overseas Service Ribbon
Marine Corps Recruiting Ribbon	Marine Corps Drill Instructor Ribbon	Marine Security Guard Ribbon
Marine Corps Reserve Ribbon	Philippine Presidential Unit Citation	Korean Presidential Unit Citation
Vietnam Presidential Unit Citation	Vietnam Gallantry Cross Unit Citation	Vietnam Civil Actions Unit Citation
Philippine Defense Ribbon	Philippine Liberation Ribbon	Philippine Independence Ribbon

Ribbon Devices

Medal of Honor Gold	Navy Cross Silver — Gold		
Defense Distinguished Service Medal Bronze	**Navy Distinguished Service Medal** Silver — Gold	**Silver Star** Silver — Gold	**Defense Superior Service Medal** Silver — Bronze
Legion of Merit Gold — Silver — Gold	**Distinguished Flying Cross** Gold — Silver — Gold	**Navy & Marine Corps Medal** Gold	**Bronze Star Medal** Gold — Silver — Gold
Purple Heart Silver — Gold	**Defense Meritorious Service Medal** Silver — Bronze	**Meritorious Service Medal** Silver — Gold	**Air Medal** Gold — Bronze — Silver — Gold
Joint Service Commendation Medal Gold — Silver — Bronze	**Navy & Marine Corps Commendation Medal** Gold — Silver — Gold	**Joint Service Achievement Medal** Silver — Bronze	**Navy & Marine Corps Achievement Medal** Gold — Silver — Gold
Combat Action Ribbon Silver — Gold	**Navy Presidential Unit Citation** Silver — Bronze	**Joint Meritorious Unit Award** Silver — Bronze	**Navy Unit Commendation** Silver — Bronze
Navy Meritorious Unit Commendation Silver — Bronze	**Navy "E" Ribbon** Silver — Silver	**Prisoner of War Medal** Silver — Bronze	**Marine Corps Good Conduct Medal** Silver — Bronze
Selected Marine Corps Reserve Medal Silver — Bronze	**Marine Corps Expeditionary Medal** Silver — Silver Bronze	**China Service Medal** Bronze	**American Defense Service Medal** Bronze — A Bronze
American Campaign Medal Bronze	**European-African-Middle Eastern Campaign** Silver — Bronze	**Asiatic-Pacific Campaign Medal** Silver — Bronze	**World War II Victory Medal** None
Navy Occupation Service Gold Airplane	**Medal For Humane Action** None	**National Defense Service Medal** Bronze	**Korean Service Medal** Silver — Bronze
Antarctica Service Medal Bronze, Gold, or Silver	**Armed Forces Expeditionary Medal** Silver — Bronze	**Vietnam Service Medal** Silver — Bronze	**Southwest Asia Service Medal** Bronze
Armed Forces Service Medal Silver — Bronze	**Humanitarian Service Medal** Silver — Bronze	**Outstanding Volunteer Service Medal** Silver — Bronze	**Navy Sea Service Deployment Ribbon** Silver — Bronze
Navy Arctic Service Ribbon None	**Navy & Marine Corps Overseas Service Ribbon** Silver — Bronze	**Marine Corps Recruiting Ribbon** Silver — Bronze	**Marine Corps Drill Instructor Ribbon** Silver — Bronze
Marine Security Guard Ribbon Silver — Bronze	**Armed Forces Reserve Medal** Bronze, Silver, Gold, Hourglass — 3 — M Bronze	**Marine Corps Reserve Ribbon (Obsolete)** None	**Foreign Decoration** As Specified by the Awarding Government
Philippine Republic Presidential Unit Citation Bronze	**Republic of Korea Presidential Unit Citation** None	**Republic of Vietnam Presidential Unit Citation** None	**Republic of Vietnam Gallantry Cross Unit Citation** Bronze Palm
Republic of Vietnam Civil Actions Unit Citation Bronze Palm	**Philippine Defense Ribbon** Bronze	**Philippine Liberation Ribbon** Bronze	**Philippine Independence Ribbon** None
United Nations Service Medal None	**United Nations Medal** Bronze	**NATO Medal** Bronze	**Multinational Force & Observers Medal** Bronze Numeral
Inter-American Defense Board Medal Gold	**Republic of Vietnam Campaign Medal** Silver Date Bar	**Kuwait Liberation Medal (Saudi Arabia)** Gold Palm Tree	**Kuwait Liberation Medal (Emirate of Kuwait)** None

 = Gold Star
Denotes second and subsequent awards of a decoration

 = Silver Star
Worn in the same manner as the gold star, in lieu of five gold stars.

 = Bronze Service Star
Denotes second and subsequent awards of a service award or participation in a campaign or major operation

 = Silver Service Star
Worn in lieu of five gold or bronze service stars

 = Bronze Oak Leaf Cluster
Denotes second and subsequent awards of a Joint Service decoration or unit citation

 = Silver Oak Leaf Cluster
Worn in lieu of five bronze oak leaf clusters

 = Gold Letter "V"
Awarded for distinguished actions in combat (valor)

 = Silver Letter "W"
Denotes participation in Defense of Wake Island

 = Bronze Letter "M"
Denotes reservists mobilized and called to active duty

 = Antarctica Disk
Denotes personnel who "wintered over" on the Antarctic continent

 = Bronze Numeral
Denotes total number of strike/flight awards of the Air Medal

 = Bronze Hourglass
Issued for each succeeding award of the Armed Forces Reserve Medal.

 = Bronze Palm
Awarded with the Vietnam Gallantry Cross Unit Citation

U.S. Marine Corps
Correct Order Of Ribbon Wear
(Left Breast)

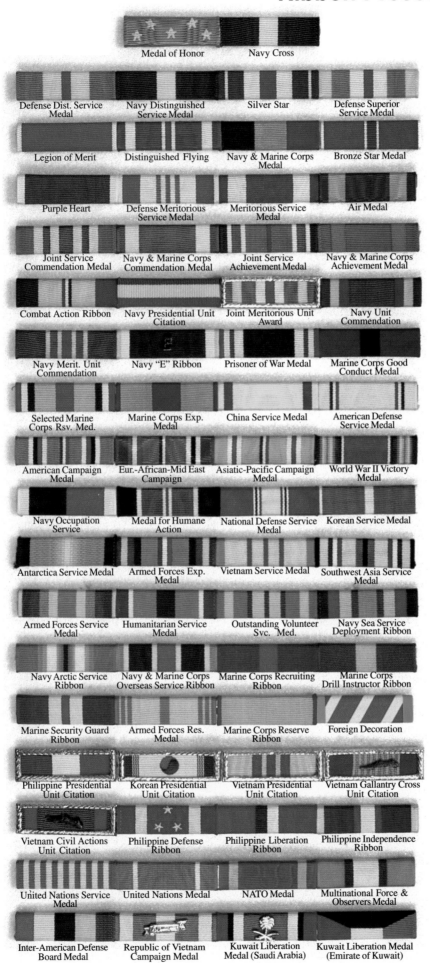

Medal of Honor   Navy Cross

Defense Dist. Service Medal | Navy Distinguished Service Medal | Silver Star | Defense Superior Service Medal

Legion of Merit | Distinguished Flying | Navy & Marine Corps Medal | Bronze Star Medal

Purple Heart | Defense Meritorious Service Medal | Meritorious Service Medal | Air Medal

Joint Service Commendation Medal | Navy & Marine Corps Commendation Medal | Joint Service Achievement Medal | Navy & Marine Corps Achievement Medal

Combat Action Ribbon | Navy Presidential Unit Citation | Joint Meritorious Unit Award | Navy Unit Commendation

Navy Merit. Unit Commendation | Navy "E" Ribbon | Prisoner of War Medal | Marine Corps Good Conduct Medal

Selected Marine Corps Rsv. Med. | Marine Corps Exp. Medal | China Service Medal | American Defense Service Medal

American Campaign Medal | Eur.-African-Mid East Campaign | Asiatic-Pacific Campaign Medal | World War II Victory Medal

Navy Occupation Service | Medal for Humane Action | National Defense Service Medal | Korean Service Medal

Antarctica Service Medal | Armed Forces Exp. Medal | Vietnam Service Medal | Southwest Asia Service Medal

Armed Forces Service Medal | Humanitarian Service Medal | Outstanding Volunteer Svc. Med. | Navy Sea Service Deployment Ribbon

Navy Arctic Service Ribbon | Navy & Marine Corps Overseas Service Ribbon | Marine Corps Recruiting Ribbon | Marine Corps Drill Instructor Ribbon

Marine Security Guard Ribbon | Armed Forces Res. Medal | Marine Corps Reserve Ribbon | Foreign Decoration

Philippine Presidential Unit Citation | Korean Presidential Unit Citation | Vietnam Presidential Unit Citation | Vietnam Gallantry Cross Unit Citation

Vietnam Civil Actions Unit Citation | Philippine Defense Ribbon | Philippine Liberation Ribbon | Philippine Independence Ribbon

United Nations Service Medal | United Nations Medal | NATO Medal | Multinational Force & Observers Medal

Inter-American Defense Board Medal | Republic of Vietnam Campaign Medal | Kuwait Liberation Medal (Saudi Arabia) | Kuwait Liberation Medal (Emirate of Kuwait)

Medals of Honor and Brevet Medal

Navy Medal of Honor
(1861)

Navy Medal of Honor
(1917-1942)

Brevet Medal
(1921)

"Tiffany Cross"
(Blue Ribbon has white stars like Navy Medal of Honor below)
Pg. 58

Pg. 8

Pg. 8

Navy Medal of Honor
(Current)

Pg. 58

Navy Cross
Pg. 59

**Defense Distinguished
Service Medal**
Pg. 59

**Navy Distinguished
Service Medal**
Pg. 60

Silver Star
Pg. 60

**Defense Superior
Service Medal**
Pg. 61

Legion Of Merit
Pg. 61

**Distinguished
Flying Cross**
Pg. 62

**Navy and Marine Corps
Medal**
Pg. 63

**Bronze Star
Medal**
Pg. 63

Purple Heart
Pg. 64

**Defense Meritorious
Service Medal**
Pg. 65

**Meritorious
Service Medal**
Pg. 65

43

U.S. Personal Decorations and Service Medals

Air Medal
Pg. 66

Joint Service Commendation Medal
Pg. 67

Navy and Marine Corps Commendation Medal
Pg. 67

Joint Service Achievement Medal
Pg. 68

Navy and Marine Corps Achievement Medal
Pg. 68

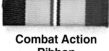

Combat Action Ribbon
Pg. 69

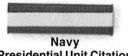

Navy Presidential Unit Citation
Pg. 69

Joint Meritorious Unit Award
Pg. 69

Navy Unit Commendation
Pg. 70

Navy Meritorious Unit Commendation
Pg. 70

Navy "E" Ribbon
Pg. 70

Prisoner of War Medal
Pg. 71

Marine Corps Good Conduct Medal
Pg. 71

Selected Marine Corps Reserve Medal
Pg. 72

Marine Corps Expeditionary Medal
Pg. 73

China Service Medal
Pg. 73

**American Defense
Service Medal
Pg. 74**

**American Campaign
Medal
Pg. 74**

**European-African- Middle
Eastern Campaign Medal
Pg. 75**

**Asiatic-Pacific
Campaign Medal
Pg. 76**

**World War II
Victory Medal
Pg. 77**

**Navy Occupation
Service Medal
Pg. 77**

**Medal for
Humane Action
Pg. 78**

**National Defense
Service Medal
Pg. 78**

**Korean Service
Medal
Pg. 79**

**Antarctica Service
Medal
Pg. 80**

**Armed Forces
Expeditionary Medal
Pg. 81**

**Vietnam Service
Medal
Pg. 82**

U.S. Service Medals and Foreign Decorations

Southwest Asia Service Medal
Pg. 83

Armed Forces Service Medal
Pg. 84

Humanitarian Service Medal
Pg. 84

Outstanding Volunteer Service Medal
Pg. 85

Navy Sea Service Deployment Ribbon
Pg. 85

Marine Corps Recruiting Ribbon
Pg. 86

Navy Arctic Service Ribbon
Pg. 86

Marine Corps Drill Instructor Ribbon
Pg. 87

Navy and Marine Corps Overseas Service Ribbon
Pg. 86

Marine Security Guard Ribbon
Pg. 87

Armed Forces Reserve Medal
Pg. 88

Marine Corps Reserve Ribbon
Pg. 88

Republic of Vietnam Staff Service Medal
(Typical Foreign Decoration) Pg. 89

Philippine Presidential Unit Citation
Pg. 89

Republic of Korea Presidential Unit Citation
Pg. 90

Republic of Vietnam Presidential Unit Citation
Pg. 90

Republic of Vietnam Gallantry Cross Unit Citation Pg. 90

Republic of Vietnam Civil Actions Unit Citation
Pg. 91

Philippine Defense Medal
Pg. 91

Foreign Decorations and Non-U.S. Service Awards

**Philippine Liberation
Medal
Pg. 92**

**Philippine
Independence Medal
Pg. 92**

**United Nations
Service Medal (Korea)
Pg. 93**

**United Nations
Medal
Pg. 93**

**NATO Medal
Pg. 96**

**Multinational Force and
Observers Medal
Pg. 96**

**Inter-American
Defense Board
Medal
Pg. 97**

**Republic of Vietnam
Campaign Medal
Pg. 97**

**Kuwait Liberation Medal
(Saudi Arabia)
Pg. 98**

**Kuwait Liberation Medal
(Emirate of Kuwait)
Pg. 98**

**50th Anniversary of WWII
Victory Medal
Pg. 105**

**Korean War Service
Commemorative
Medal
Pg. 105**

47

Examples of Ribbons, Medals and Lapel Pins

Before the Korean War, Navy and Marine ribbons were ½ inch high and 1⅓ inch long. After Korea all Armed Forces ribbons became ⅜ inch high and 1⅜ inch long.

Marine Ribbons (WWI Style)

Marine Ribbons (WWII Style)

Marine Ribbons Covered in Plastic (WWII Style)

Army/Air Force Ribbons Covered in Plastic (WWII Style)

Korean Era Ribbons Covered in Plastic

Vietnam Era Ribbons

Purple Heart Ribbon (1932-1955)

Purple Heart Ribbon (Current)

Lapel Pin

Marine Corps Good Conduct Medal (Old Style)

Marine Corps Good Conduct Medal (Current)

Miniature Medal

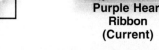

Medals Mounted for Wear (side by side)

Civilian Hat Pin

Lapel Pins for Button Hole (Old Style)

Medals Mounted for Wear
Maximum 7 Medals to a Bar
(Overlapped)

Combat Action

NPUC

Purple Heart

WW II Victory

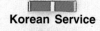

Korean Service

Vietnam Service

NDS

Lapel Pin (New Style)

48

Examples of Award Displays

World War II

The 2nd Marine Division Patch is topped by an Officer's Cap Insignia and flanked by Captain's Rank Insignia. The Medals shown are: Bronze Star, Purple Heart, American Campaign, Asiatic-Pacific Campaign, WWII Victory, Navy Occupation and the 50th Anniversary of WWII Medals. Marksmanship Badges and an Honorable Discharge Pin are displayed adjacent to a name plate.

Pacific Service

A Marine Blazer Emblem is flanked by Corporal's Chevrons and Dress Collar Insignia. The Medals shown are: Bronze Star, Purple Heart, Good Conduct, American Defense, American Campaign, Asiatic-Pacific, WW II Victory and 2 Commemorative Medals. A name plate is flanked by Marksmanship Badges.

Vietnam Service

Rank and Cap Insignia are displayed above the Bronze Star, Purple Heart, Navy Commendation, National Defense Service, Vietnam Service, RVN Civil Actions, RVN Campaign Medals and a Commemorative Medal. The Combat Action Ribbon and Navy PUC are shown above a name plate and Marksmanship Badges.

Korean Service

Dress Collar Insignia and the 1st Marine Division Patch are displayed above the Good Conduct, National Defense Service, Korean Service, UN Korean Service and Korean Service Commemorative Medals. Displayed below are the Navy and Korean Presidential Unit Citations above a name plate and Marksmanship Badges.

Southwest Asia

A Marine Medallion and Dress Collar Insignia are displayed above Ribbons and Medals. The Medals are: Navy Achievement, Good Conduct, National Defense Service, Southwest Asia Service and Saudi & Kuwait Liberation Medals. The Ribbon set also includes the Sea Service and Overseas Service Ribbons, which are ribbon only awards.

Peacetime Service

Rank and Cap Insignia are displayed over Ribbons and Medals. The Medals are: Navy Achievement, Good Conduct, National Defense Service, Armed Forces Expeditionary, Armed Forces and Humanitarian Service and UN Medals. The Ribbon set also includes the Sea Service and Overseas Service Ribbons which are ribbons only awards.

49

Rank Insignia and Service Stripes

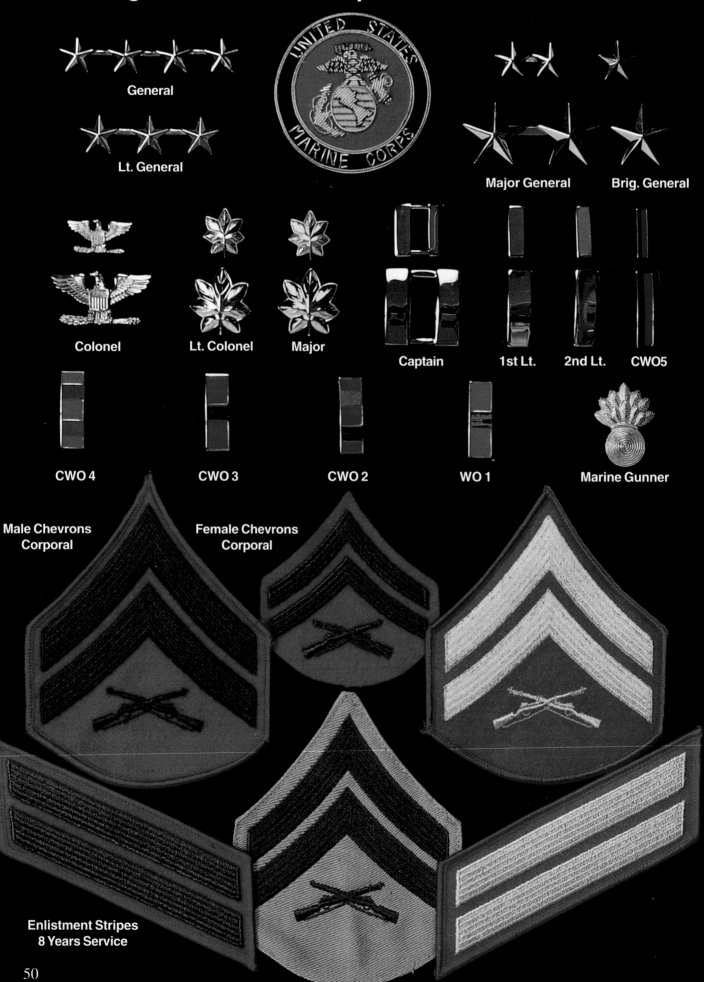

General

Lt. General

Major General

Brig. General

Colonel

Lt. Colonel

Major

Captain

1st Lt.

2nd Lt.

CWO5

CWO 4

CWO 3

CWO 2

WO 1

Marine Gunner

Male Chevrons
Corporal

Female Chevrons
Corporal

Enlistment Stripes
8 Years Service

50

Naval Aviator   **(Miniature)**

Navy/Marine Corps Parachutist

Balloon Pilot

Basic Parachutist

Naval Flight Officer

Master Explosive Ordnance Disposal (EOD)

Naval Astronaut Aviator

Senior Explosive Ordnance Disposal (EOD)

Naval Astronaut Flight Officer

Basic Explosive Ordnance Disposal (EOD)

Marine Aerial Navigator

Scuba Diver

Naval Aviation Observer

Naval Aircrewman

Combat Aircrew

Uniform Insignia and Marksmanship Badges

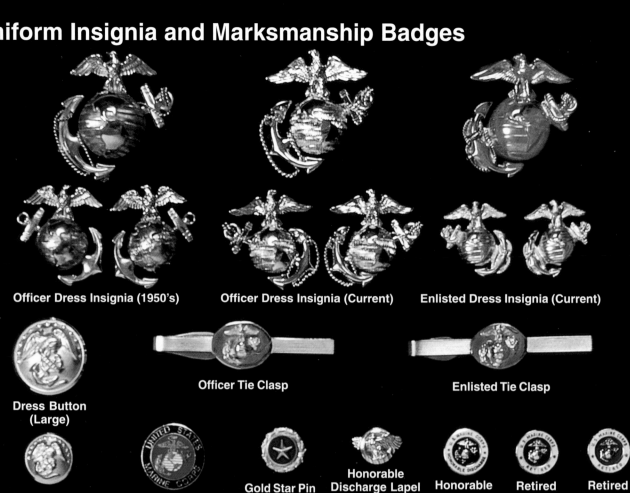

Officer Dress Insignia (1950's)

Officer Dress Insignia (Current)

Enlisted Dress Insignia (Current)

Dress Button
(Large)

Officer Tie Clasp

Enlisted Tie Clasp

Dress Button
(Small)

Lapel Pin

Gold Star Pin
Button

Honorable
Discharge Lapel
Pin (WWII)

Honorable
Discharge
Lapel Pin

Retired
Lapel Pin
(20 Years)

Retired
Lapel Pin
(30 years)

Expert Rifleman
Badge (Obsolete)

Basic Badge
(Obsolete)

"Q" Bars (Obsolete)

Rifle Expert
Badge

Pistol Expert
Badge

Sharpshooter
Badge - Rifle (Obsolete)

Sharpshooter
Badge - Pistol
(Obsolete)

Rifle Sharpshooter

Pistol
Sharpshooter

Marksman Badge - Rifle
(Obsolete)

Rifle Marksman Badge

Pistol Marksman
Badge

52

Service/Identification and Trophy Badges

**Presidential
Service Badge**

**Secretary of Defense
ID Badge**

**Joint Chiefs of Staff
ID Badge**

**Miniature JCS
ID Badge**

**Marine Corps
Distinguished
Marksman**

**Marine Corps
Distinguished
Pistol Shot**

**Marine Corps
Pistol Championship
(Walsh Trophy)**

**Marine Corps
Inter-Division
Rifle Competition
(Gold)**

**Marine Corps
Rifle Competition (Gold)**

**Marine Corps
Rifle Competition (Silver)**

**Marine Corps
Rifle Competition (Bronze)**

**Marine Corps
Pistol Competition
(Silver)**

**Marine Corps
Pistol Competition
(Bronze)**

**Marine Corps
Division Rifle Competition
(Silver)**

**Marine Corps
Division Rifle Competition
(Gold)**

53

Shoulder Patches

1st Marine
Division

2nd Marine
Division (Early Design)

2nd Marine
Division

3rd Marine
Division

4th Marine
Division

5th Marine
Brigade (WW I)

5th Marine
Division

6th Marine
Division

4th Marine
Air Wing (Early Design)

13th Marine
Defense Bn.

18th Marine
Defense Bn.

51st Defense Bn.

52nd Defense Bn.

Marine Ship
Detachment Afloat
"Sea Marines"

Marine Detachment
Londonberry

1st Marine Brigade
(Iceland)

Pacific Air Wing
Headquarters

1st Marine Air Wing

2nd Marine Air Wing

3rd Marine Air Wing

4th Marine Air Wing

FMF Honor Guard

FMF Pacific HQ.

FMF Pacific
Engineer Bn.

FMF Pacific
Supply

54

Shoulder Patches

FMF Pacific
Pacific DUKW Co.

FMF Pacific
Artillery Bn.

FMF Pacific
Anti-Aircraft Art.

FMF Pacific
Tractor Bn.

FMF Pacific Bomb
Disposal Co.

FMF Pacific
Dog Platoon

1st M.A.C.
Headquarters

1st M.A.C. Arty.

1st M.A.C. Aviation
Engineers

1st M.A.C. Barrage
Balloon Bn.

1st M.A.C. Defense Bn.

1st M.A.C.
Paratroops

1st M.A.C. Raiders

1st M.A.C. Service
Supply Bn.

3rd Amphibious
Corps

5th Amphibious
Corps

704th Marine
Raider Bn.

Marine Aircraft HQ
Pacific Wings

Aircraft
Fuselage
1st Wing

Aircraft
Fuselage
2nd Wing

Aircraft Fuselage
3rd Wing

Aircraft Fuselage
4th Wing

1st Marine Brigade
Fleet Marine Force

U.S.M.C.
Unofficial

Decorations and Awards

Young Marines of the  Marine Corps League

Tel: (202) 889-8745
(202) 889-2720
FAX: (202) 889-0502

Young Marine National Headquarters
P.O Box 70735
Southwest Station
Washington, D.C. 20024-0735

Personal Decorations

Distinguished Service Adult #1430	Distinguished Service Young Marine #1107	Adult of the Year #2054	Young Marine of the Year #1336	Personal Commendation #1311

Meritorious Service #1528	Lifesaving/1st Degree #1293	Lifesaving/2nd Degree #1301	Lifesaving/3rd Degree #2090	Personal Achievement #1335

Commendation of Merit #1200	Honor Recruit #4030

Service Awards

Distinguished Unit Citation/ National #5026	Meritorious Unit/Nat'l Citation #1193	Meritorious Unit/Division Commendation #1192	Meritorious Unit/Regt. Commendation #1191	Marine Corps League Commendation #1502

Good Conduct #1543	National Staff #1533	Division Staff #1500	Regimental Staff #1490	Battalion Staff #1423

Unit Commanders #1494	Platoon Commanders #1309	Color Guard #1221	Attendance/Adult #1225	Attendance/Young Marine #1226

Qualification Awards

Platoon Leaders Course #5023	Leadership #1384	Academic Achievement #1223	Drug Demand Reduction #5024	Outstanding Salesmanship #5009

Physical Fitness #1105	Sportsmanship #1168	Musicians #1121	Advanced First Aid #1106	Qualified Corpsman #1501

C.P.R. #1346	Swimming #1168	Seamanship #1213	Scuba #1250	Advanced Field #9925

Qualified Field #1544	Orienteering #1182	Communication #1535	Conservation #1525	Marksmanship #1117

Achievement #1205	Community Service #1224	Basic #1119	Drill Team Competition #1129	Drill Team #1130

National Encampment #1506	Division Encampment #1504	Regiment Encampment #1505	Battalion Encampment #1503	Organized Unit Trip #1108

Compliments of
Drug Enforcement Administration
Washington Field Division

Printed by Medals of America
1929 Fairview Rd., Fountain Inn, SC

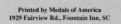

(Revised 1994)

Service and Utility Uniform Insignia

Officer Service Insignia
(1950's)

Officer Service Insignia
(Current)

Enlisted Service Insignia
(Current)

Service Buttons
(Current)

Officer Lapel Insignia
(WWII)

Enlisted Service
Buttons
(1950's)

EOD Utility Insignia

Hospital Corpsman
Utility Insignia

Dental Technician
Utility Insignia

Marine Gunner
Service Insignia

Sergeant Major
Utility Insignia

Master Gunnery
Sergeant Utility Insignia

First Sergeant
Utility Insignia

Master Sergeant
Utility Insignia

Gunnery Sergeant
Utility Insignia

Staff Sergeant
Utility Insignia

Sergeant
Utility Insignia

Corporal
Utility Insignia

Lance Corporal
Utility Insignia

Private First Class
Utility Insignia

MEDAL OF HONOR
(Navy-Marine Corps-Coast Guard Design)

*Navy Medal of Honor
(1861)*

*Navy Medal of Honor
"Tiffany Cross" (1919-1942)*

*Navy Medal of Honor
(1942-Present)*

"For conspicuous gallantry and intrepidity at the risk of life, above and beyond the call of duty, in action, involving actual conflict with an opposing armed force." The Medal of Honor is worn before all other decorations and medals and is the highest honor that can be conferred on a member of the Armed Forces. Since its inception, 3,427 Medal of Honor have been awarded to 3,408 individuals, 249 to Marines.

The Medal of Honor was signed into law by President Lincoln on 21 December 1861. This Public Resolution 82 contained a provision for a Navy medal of valor. At first the decoration was intended to recognize gallantry in action by enlisted personnel, but was later amended to include officers. Congress also passed an act on 9 July 1918 which established criteria for the award that the act of heroism had to be above and beyond the call of duty and so unique as to clearly distinguish the recipient from his comrades.

In 1919 the so called "Tiffany Cross" Medal of Honor version came into use and remained until 1942, when the current Navy Medal of Honor was instituted. This version was often referred to as the "Tiffany Cross," since Tiffany was involved with its design. The medal was a gold cross patee on a wreath of oak and laurel leaves. In the center of the cross was an octagon with the inscriptionUNITED STATES NAVY 1917-1919. Inside the octagon was an eagle design of the United States Seal and an anchor appeared on each arm of the cross. The reverse of the medal had the raised inscription AWARDED TO and space for the recipient's name. The medal was suspended by a light blue ribbon with thirteen white stars. The ribbon was suspended from a rectangular gold pin bar inscribed with the words VALOUR.

Many Americans today are confused with the term "Congressional Medal of Honor," when, in fact, the proper

term is "Medal of Honor." A law passed in July 1918 authorized the President to present the medal in the name of Congress. Part of this confusion stems from the fact that all MOH recipients belong to the Congressional Medal of Honor Society chartered by Congress.

An act of Congress in July 1963 clarified and amended the criteria for awarding the Medal of Honor to prevent award of the medal for deeds done "in line of profession," but not necessarily in actual conflict with an enemy. This act of Congress made the clarification by stating that the award was "for service in military operations involving conflict with an opposing force or for such service with friendly forces engaged in armed conflict."

A recommendation for the Navy Medal of Honor must be made within three years from the date of the deed upon which it depends and award of the medal must be made within five years after the date of the deed. A stipulation for the medal is that there must be a minimum of two witnesses to the deed, who swear separately that the event transpired as stated in the final citation.

The current Navy Medal of Honor has been revised three times and has been in its current form since August 1942. The medal is a five pointed star with a standing figure of the Goddess Minerva surrounded by a circle of stars representing the number of States in the Union at the outbreak of the Civil War. Minerva, the Goddess of Strength and Wisdom, holds a shield taken from the Great Seal of the United States, and in her left hand she holds a fasces, which represents the lawful authority of the state; she is warding off a crouching figure representing Discord. The medal is suspended from an anchor and the reverse is plain for engraving the recipient's name. The ribbon is light blue and has an eight-sided central pad with thirteen white stars.

NAVY CROSS

Silver

Gold

Instituted: 1919
Criteria: Extraordinary heroism in action against an enemy of the U.S. while engaged in military operations involving conflict with an opposing foreign force or while serving with friendly foreign forces
Devices: Gold, silver star
Notes: Originally issued with a 1-1/2" wide ribbon

For extraordinary heroism in connection with military operations against an opposing armed force. The Navy Cross is worn after the Medal of Honor and before all other decorations.

The Navy Cross was established by an Act of Congress and approved on 4 February 1919. Initially the Navy Cross was awarded for extraordinary heroism or distinguished service in either combat or peacetime. The criteria was upgraded in August 1942 to limit the award to those individuals demonstrating extraordinary heroism in connection with military operations against an armed enemy.

The Navy Cross medal is a cross patee with the ends of the cross rounded. It has four laurel leaves with berries in each re-entrant angle, which symbolizes victory. In the center of the cross is a sailing ship on waves. The ship is a caravel, symbolic of ships of the fourteenth century. On the reverse are crossed anchors with cables attached with the letters USN amid the anchors. The ribbon is navy blue with a white center stripe. Additional awards of the Navy Cross are denoted by gold stars five-sixteenths of an inch in diameter.

DEFENSE DISTINGUISHED SERVICE MEDAL

Silver

Bronze

Instituted: 1970
Criteria: Exceptionally meritorious service to the United States while assigned to a Joint Activity in a position of unique and great responsibility
Devices: Bronze & silver oak leaf cluster

For award by the Secretary of Defense for exceptionally meritorious service in a duty of great responsibility. The Defense Distinguished Service Medal is worn after the Navy Cross and before the Navy Distinguished Service Medal.

The Defense Distinguished Service Medal was established by an Executive Order, which was signed by President Nixon on 9 July 1970. The medal was instituted for senior officers who held positions of authority over elements of other service branches. This eliminated the need to award multiple Distinguished Service Medals from the service branches involved. The medal is the highest award for meritorious service within the Department of Defense.

The Defense Distinguished Service Medal was designed by the Army's Institute of Heraldry and is gold in color featuring a blue enameled pentagon superimposed by a gold eagle with outspread wings. On the eagle's breast is the seal of the United States and in its talons are three arrows. The eagle and pentagon are surrounded by a gold circle consisting of thirteen stars and laurel and olive branches. At the top of the circle are five gold rays extending above the stars, which form the medal suspension. On the reverse of the pentagon is the raised inscription FROM THE SECRETARY OF DEFENSE TO, with a space for inscribing the recipient's name. On the reverse of the gold circle is the raised inscription FOR DISTINGUISHED SERVICE. The ribbon has a narrow red center stripe flanked on either side by stripes of gold and blue. Additional awards of the Defense Distinguished Service Medal are denoted by oak leaf clusters.

NAVY DISTINGUISHED SERVICE MEDAL

Silver

Gold

Instituted: 1919

Criteria: Exceptionally meritorious service to the U.S. Government in a duty of great responsibility

Devices: Gold, silver star

Notes: 107 copies of earlier medal design issued but later withdrawn. First ribbon design was 1 1/2" wide

For exceptionally meritorious service to the Government in a duty of great responsibility. The Navy Distinguished Service Medal is worn after the Defense Distinguished Service Medal and before the Silver Star.

The Navy Distinguished Service Medal was established by an Act of Congress and approved on 4 February 1919 and, like the Navy Cross, was made retroactive to 6 April 1917. During this period there was confusion about what criteria constituted the award of the Navy Distinguished Service Medal and what criteria constituted the award of the Navy Cross. At the outbreak of World War II laws governing the award of naval decorations were changed with Public Law 702, which placed the Navy Cross above the Navy Distinguished Service Medal and clearly limited the Navy Distinguished Service Medal for exceptionally meritorious service and not for acts of heroism. The very first Navy Distinguished Service Medal was awarded, posthumously, to Brigadier General Charles M. Doyen, USMC.

The Navy Distinguished Service Medal is a gold medallion with an American bald eagle with displayed wings in the center. The eagle is surrounded by a blue enameled ring which contains the words, UNITED STATES OF AMERICA with NAVY at the bottom. Outside the blue ring is a gold border of waves. The medal is suspended from its ribbon by a five pointed white enameled star with an anchor in the center. Behind the star are gold rays emanating from the re-entrant angles of the star. The reverse of the medal contains a trident surrounded by a wreath of laurel. The wreath is surrounded by a blue enamel ring with the inscription FOR DISTINGUISHED SERVICE. The blue enamel ring is surrounded by a gold border of waves the same as on the front of the medal. The ribbon is navy blue with a gold stripe in the center. Additional awards of the Navy Distinguished Service Medal are denoted by gold stars five sixteenths of an inch in diameter.

SILVER STAR

Silver

Gold

Instituted: 1932

Criteria: Gallantry in action against an armed enemy of the United States or while serving with friendly foreign forces

Devices: Gold, silver star

Notes: Derived from the 3/16" silver "Citation Star" previously worn on Army campaign medals

For gallantry in action (1) against an enemy of the United States; (2) while engaged in military operations involving conflict with an opposing foreign force; or, (3) while serving with friendly foreign forces engaged in armed conflict with an opposing foreign force in which the United States is not a belligerent party. The required gallantry, while of a lesser degree than required for the award of the Navy Cross, must nevertheless have been performed with marked distinction. The Silver Star is worn after the Navy Distinguished Service Medal and before the Defense Superior Service Medal.

The Silver Star was originally established by President Woodrow Wilson on 9 July 1918 as a three-sixteenth inch silver citation star to be worn on the World War I Victory Medal to denote receipt of a special letter of commendation. Although the citation star was widely used during World War I, it was not a popular award. Arguments centered around the fact that the award was "insignificant in size and constitutes very little tangible evidence of gallantry, is not an article which can be handed down to posterity and, therefore, serve as evidence of a grateful nation and people with attendant stimulation to patriotism." Because of these arguments, the Army decided to redesign the citation star by placing it on a medal. The medal as it is today was created in 1932 for the Army and extended to the Navy and Marine Corps on 8 August 1942.

The medal was designed by Bailey, Banks and Biddle, an Atlanta retail jeweler. The medal is a five pointed gilt-bronze star with a small silver star centered in the middle, which is actually a representation of the original citation star. The small silver star is surrounded by a laurel wreath with rays radiating outward from the star. The reverse of the medal has the raised inscription FOR GALLANTRY IN ACTION and room for inscribing the recipient's name. The ribbon, employing the colors of the American Flag, has a wide red center stripe flanked on either side by a wide white stripe, a wide dark blue stripe, a thin white stripe and a thin dark blue stripe at the edges. Additional awards are denoted by five-sixteenth inch diameter gold stars.

DEFENSE SUPERIOR SERVICE MEDAL

Silver

Bronze

Instituted: 1976
Criteria: Superior meritorious service to the United States while assigned to a Joint Activity in a position of significant responsibility
Devices: Bronze, silver oak leaf cluster

For award by the Secretary of Defense for superior meritorious service while in a position of significant responsibility while assigned to a joint activity. The Defense Superior Service Medal is worn after the Silver Star and before the Legion of Merit.

The Defense Superior Service Medal was established by an Executive Order, which was signed by President Ford on 6 February 1976. The medal was instituted to recognize duty performed with distinction and significance that would justify an award comparable to the Legion of Merit for members of the Armed Forces assigned to the Office of the Secretary of Defense and other activities in the Department of Defense.

The Defense Superior Service Medal was designed by the Army's Institute of Heraldry and is of the same design as the Defense Distinguished Service Medal. The medal is silver in color featuring a blue enameled pentagon superimposed by a gold eagle with outspread wings. On the eagle's breast is the seal of the United States and in its talons are three arrows. The eagle and pentagon are surrounded by a silver circle consisting of thirteen stars and laurel and olive branches. At the top of the circle are five silver rays extending above the stars, which form the medal suspension. On the reverse of the pentagon is the raised inscription FROM THE SECRETARY OF DEFENSE TO with space to inscribe the recipient's name. On the back is the inscription FOR SUPERIOR SERVICE. The ribbon consists of a central stripe of red flanked on either side by stripes of white, blue and yellow. Additional awards of the Defense Superior Service Medal are denoted by oak leaf clusters.

LEGION OF MERIT

Gold

Silver

Gold

Instituted: 1942
Criteria: Exceptionally meritorious conduct in the performance of outstanding services to the United States
Devices: Bronze letter "V" (for valor), gold, silver star
Notes: Issued in four degrees (Legionnaire, Officer, Commander & Chief Commander) to foreign nationals

For exceptionally meritorious conduct in the performance of outstanding service. The Legion of Merit is worn after the Defense Superior Service Medal and before the Distinguished Flying Cross.

The Legion of Merit was established by an Act of Congress, which was approved 20 July 1942 and signed by President Franklin D. Roosevelt on 29 October 1942. The medal was instituted to fill the gap below the Distinguished Service Medal and provide an award that could be given for meritorious service in positions of considerable responsibility but below the positions of great responsibility called for by the criteria of the Distinguished Service Medal.

The Legion of Merit was designed by Colonel Townsend Heard and followed the basic design of the French Legion of Honor. The medal is a white enameled five-armed cross with ten gold tipped points. The cross is bordered in red enamel. In the center of the cross there is a blue enameled circle with thirteen stars surrounded by a border of gold clouds. Behind the cross is a gold circle bordered by a laurel wreath that is tied in a bow between the two lower arms of the cross. Gold crossed arrows appear between each of the arms of the cross. The same cross appears on the reverse of the medal except there is no enamel. In the center of the reverse is a rope circle for engraving the recipient's name. Contained in a second rope circle is

Continued on page 62

LEGION OF MERIT *continued from page 61*

the raised inscription ANNUIT COEPTIS MDCCLXXXII. The words ANNUIT COEPTIS are Latin meaning "God has favored our undertaking" and comes from the Great Seal of the United States. The MDCCLXXXII (1782) refers to the date George Washington founded the Badge of Military Merit, from which the Legion of Merit evolved. There is an outer ribbon circle with the raised inscription UNITED STATES OF AMERICA. The ribbon is ruby (pinkish-red) edged in white. Additional awards are denoted by five-sixteenth inch gold stars. A Combat Distinguishing Device (Combat "V") may be authorized.

The Legion of Merit is awarded in four degrees to foreign nationals:

Chief Commander of the Legion of Merit, the highest degree, is intended for the heads of state of friendly foreign militaries. The medal is in the form of a three inch diameter breast star. The service ribbon features a gold miniature of the medal set on a gold-colored bar engraved with two rows of arrow feathers on a ruby red ribbon edged in white.

Commander of the Legion of Merit, the second degree, is intended for high ranking officers of friendly foreign militaries. The medal is suspended from a neck ribbon of the same color and design as the ribbon bar. The service ribbon features a silver miniature of the medal set on a silver-colored bar engraved with two rows of arrow feathers on a ruby red ribbon edged in white.

Officer of the Legion of Merit, the third degree, is intended for field grade officers of friendly foreign militaries. The medal is identical to the Legionnaire grade with the addition of an eleven-sixteenth inch gold-colored miniature of the planchet (medal) attached to the suspension ribbon. The service ribbon has a five-sixteenth inch gold-colored miniature of the planchet (medal) on a ruby red ribbon edged in white.

Legionnaire of the Legion of Merit, the fourth degree, is conferred upon friendly foreign service members and members of the Armed Forces of the United States. The Legion of Merit is commonly used to recognize field grade officers and Sergeants Major upon their retirement. The Legion of Merit is the second highest peacetime award behind the Distinguished Service Medals.

DISTINGUISHED FLYING CROSS

Gold   Silver   Gold

Instituted: 1926
Criteria: Heroism or extraordinary achievement while participating in aerial flight
Devices: Bronze letter "V" (for valor), gold, silver star

For heroism or extraordinary achievement while participating in aerial flight. The Distinguished Flying Cross is worn after the Legion of Merit and before the Navy and Marine Corps Medal.

The Distinguished Flying Cross was established by an Act of Congress and approved in July 1926. The Act of Congress was implemented in January 1927 by President Coolidge. If the medal is awarded for an act of heroism, the act must involve voluntary action in the face of danger and be above the actions of others in a similar operation. If awarded for extraordinary achievement, it must have resulted in an accomplishment so outstanding or exceptional that the act clearly sets the individual apart from his or her comrades. This is specifically an aviation award.

The Distinguished Flying Cross was designed by the Army's Institute of Heraldry and is a bronze four bladed propeller surmounted on a bronze cross pattee. Behind the cross are bronze rays forming a square. The medal is suspended from a plain bronze suspender. The back of the medal is blank to allow for engraving the recipient's name. The ribbon is blue with a red center stripe bordered in white. The ribbon is outlined with a white stripe on each side. Additional awards are denoted by five-sixteenth inch diameter gold stars. The Combat Distinguishing Device (Combat "V") may be authorized for qualifying service rendered after 4 April 1974.

NAVY AND MARINE CORPS MEDAL

Silver Gold

Instituted: 1942
Criteria: Heroism not involving actual conflict with an armed enemy of the United States
Devices: Gold, silver star
Notes: For acts of life-saving, action must be at great risk to one's own life

For heroism that involves the voluntary risk of life under conditions other than those of conflict with an opposing armed force. The Navy and Marine Corps Medal is worn after the Distinguished Flying Cross and before the Bronze Star Medal.

The Navy and Marine Corps Medal was established by an Act of Congress and approved on 7 August 1942. The medal was established to recognize non-combat heroism. For acts of lifesaving, or attempted lifesaving, it is required that the action be performed at the risk of one's own life. The Navy and Marine Corps Medal is prized above many combat decorations by Marines who have received it.

The Navy and Marine Corps Medal was designed by Lt. Commander McClelland Barclay, USNR. The medal is a bronze octagon with an eagle perched upon a fouled anchor. Beneath the anchor is a globe and below that the inscription HEROISM in raised letters. The back of the medal is blank to allow for engraving the recipient's name. The ribbon consists of three equal strips of Navy blue, gold and scarlet. Additional awards are denoted by five-sixteenth inch gold stars.

BRONZE STAR MEDAL

Gold Silver Gold

Instituted: 1944
Criteria: Heroic or meritorious achievement or service not involving participation in aerial flight
Devices: Bronze letter "V" (for valor), gold, silver star

For heroic or meritorious achievement or service, not involving aerial flight in connection with operations against an opposing armed force. The Bronze Star Medal is worn after the Navy and Marine Corps Medal and before the Purple Heart.

The Bronze Star Medal was established by Executive Order and signed by President Franklin D. Roosevelt on 4 February 1944. The medal was instituted to provide ground forces with a medal comparable to the Air Medal and it was originally proposed as the "Ground Medal".

Like the Silver Star, the Bronze Star Medal was designed by the Atlanta retail jeweler, Bailey, Banks and Biddle. Its design reflects the intent that it be a companion to the Silver Star. The medal is a bronze five pointed star with a smaller raised and centered bronze star three-sixteenths inches in diameter. The reverse of the medal has the raised inscription HEROIC OR MERITORIOUS ACHIEVEMENT forming a circle in the center. The ribbon is red with a narrow blue center stripe. A thin white stripe borders the ribbon and the blue center stripe. Additional awards are denoted by five-sixteenth inch diameter gold stars. The combat distinguishing device (Combat "V") may be authorized.

PURPLE HEART

Silver   Gold

Instituted: 1932
Criteria: Awarded to any member of the U.S. Armed Forces killed or wounded in an armed conflict
Devices: Gold, silver star

For wounds or death as a result of an act of any opposing armed force, as a result of an international terrorist attack or as a result of military operations while serving as a part of a peacekeeping force. The Purple Heart is worn after the Bronze Star Medal and before the Defense Meritorious Service Medal.

The Purple Heart stems from the Badge of Military Merit established by George Washington in 1782, which is the oldest American military decoration. Washington's Badge of Military Merit was referred to as the "Purple Heart" and was awarded for military merit. It is believed that the name comes from a wood called "purple heart", which is a smooth-grained plum-colored wood used with firearms and artillery. The wood was considered the best in the world for making gun carriages and mortar beds, because it could withstand extreme stress. The original medal was a heart-shaped purple cloth embroidered in silver with a wreath surrounding the word MERIT. It was designed by Pierre Charles L'Enfant in accordance with Washington's personal instructions. The Badge of Military Merit or "Purple Heart" though intended to be permanent, fell into disuse shortly after the Revolution and was all but forgotten as a military decoration.

The current Purple Heart Medal was revived by the War Department on 22 February 1932 at the urging of Army Chief of Staff, General Douglas MacArthur, who was also the first recipient. The medal was authorized for the Navy and Marine Corps by the Department of the Navy on 21 January 1943. Although the Purple Heart was awarded for meritorious service between 1932 and 1943, the primary purpose was to recognize those who received wounds while in the service of the United States Military. With the development of awards such as the Legion of Merit, the use of the Purple Heart came to be strictly limited to injuries sustained in combat. The current criteria states that it is to be awarded for wounds received while serving in any capacity with one of the U.S. Armed Forces after 5 April, 1917. The wounds may have been received in combat against an enemy, while a member of a peacekeeping force, while a Prisoner of War, as a result of a terrorist attack, or as a result of a friendly fire incident in hostile territory. The 1996 Defense Authorization Act extended eligibility for the Purple Heart to prisoners of war before 25 April 1962; 1962 legislation had only authorized the medal to POWs after 25 April 1962. Wounds that qualify must have required treatment by a medical officer or must be a matter of official record.

The Purple Heart was designed by the Army's Institute of Heraldry from a design originally submitted by General Douglas MacArthur and modeled by John Sinnock, Chief Engraver at the Philadelphia Mint. The medal is a purple heart with a bronze gilt border and a bronze profile of George Washington in the center. Above the heart is a shield from George Washington's Coat of Arms between two sprays of green enameled leaves. On the back of the medal, below the Coat of Arms and leaves, there is a raised bronze heart with the raised inscription FOR MILITARY MERIT and room to inscribe the name of the recipient. Initially the medals were numbered, but this practice was discontinued in July 1943 as a cost-cutting measure. The ribbon is purple edged in white. Additional awards are denoted by five-sixteenth inch diameter gold stars.

1782 Badge of Military Merit

DEFENSE MERITORIOUS SERVICE MEDAL

Silver

Bronze

Instituted: 1977
Criteria: Noncombat meritorious achievement or service while assigned to the Joint Activity
Devices: Bronze, silver oak leaf cluster

Awarded in the name of the Secretary of Defense for recognition of non-combat meritorious achievement or exceptional service while serving in a joint activity. The Defense Meritorious Service Medal is worn after the Purple Heart and before the Meritorious Service Medal.

The Defense Meritorious Service Medal was established by Executive Order, which was signed by President Carter on 3 November 1977. The medal was instituted to recognize non-combat meritorious achievement or meritorious service by members of the Armed Forces assigned to the Office of the Secretary of Defense and other activities in the Department of Defense.

The Defense Meritorious Service Medal was designed by the Army's Institute of Heraldry and is similar in design to the Defense Distinguished Service Medal. The medal is bronze in color featuring a pentagon superimposed by an eagle with outspread wings. The eagle and pentagon are surrounded by a circular wreath of laurel. The reverse is inscribed in raised letters DEFENSE MERITORIOUS SERVICE set in three lines; around the bottom are the words UNITED STATES OF AMERICA. The ribbon is white with three blue center stripes and ruby-red border stripes. Additional awards of the Defense Meritorious Service Medal are denoted by oak leaf clusters.

MERITORIOUS SERVICE MEDAL

Silver

Gold

Instituted: 1969
Criteria: Outstanding noncombat meritorious achievement or service to the United States
Devices: Gold, silver star

For outstanding non-combat meritorious achievement or service to the United States. The Meritorious Service Medal is worn after the Defense Meritorious Service Medal and before the Air Medal.

The Meritorious Service Medal was established by Executive Order and signed by President Lyndon B. Johnson on 16 January 1969. The medal is considered a peacetime equivalent to the Bronze Star Medal.

The Meritorious Service Medal was designed by the Army's Institute of Heraldry. The medal is bronze with the upper part of the medal showing the upper half of a five-pointed star with six rays emanating outward.

The lower half of the medal shows an eagle with outstretched wings standing upon laurel branches forming the bottom of the medal. The reverse consists of the raised inscription UNITED STATES OF AMERICA around the top and MERITORIOUS SERVICE at the bottom; the center is blank allowing for the inscription of the recipient's name. The ribbon is ruby red with white border stripes. Additional awards are denoted by five-sixteenth inch diameter gold stars.

AIR MEDAL

Gold   Bronze   Silver   Gold

<u>Instituted</u>: 1942
<u>Criteria</u>: Heroic actions or meritorious service while participating in aerial flight
<u>Devices</u>: Bronze letter "V" (for valor), bronze numeral, gold numeral, bronze star, gold, silver star

For meritorious achievement while participating in aerial flight. The Air Medal may be awarded to individuals who, while serving in any capacity with the Armed Forces, distinguish themselves by heroism, outstanding achievement, or by meritorious service while participating in aerial flight, but to a lesser degree than which justifies the award of the Distinguished Flying Cross. The Air Medal is worn after the Bronze Star Medal and before the Joint Service Commendation Medal. The Air Medal is considered by many to be the air version of the Bronze Star Medal.

The Air Medal was established by Executive Order , which was signed by President Franklin D. Roosevelt on 11 May 1942. The medal was intended to protect the prestige of the Distinguished Flying Cross and as a morale booster to recognize the same kind of acts that were recognized by the Distinguished Flying Cross, but to a lesser degree. The Navy and Marine Corps also use a system for awarding the medal for meritorious achievement while participating in <u>sustained aerial flight</u> operations based on the number of strikes or flights. Strikes are defined as sorties which encounter enemy opposition and flights are sorties without enemy opposition. The requirement calls for 10 strikes ,or 20 flights, or 50 missions, or 250 hours in direct combat support or any combination. The combination requires the accumulation of 20 points on the formula of a strike being valued at 2 points, a flight at 1 point , and a mission at .4 points. The Navy and Marine Corps distinguish between the award of the medal on a Strike/Flight basis and those awarded for Single Mission/Individual basis. This is done by placing a bronze arabic numeral (indicating the number of awards) on the ribbon bar on the wearer's left if the award is for Strike/Flight. If the award is for individual heroism or achievement a three-sixteenth inch bronze star is placed in the center of the ribbon for the first award, while five-sixteenth inch gold stars are used to denote additional individual awards (a silver star is used in lieu of five gold stars).

The use of stars to denote the number of Air Medals for Single Mission/Individual awards was discontinued during the period from 1 January 1980 to 22 November 1989 and a practice of using gold arabic numerals (indicating the number of awards) on the ribbon bar on the wearer's RIGHT was substituted. The current practice (since 22 November 1989) of denoting the number of Air Medals for Single Mission/Individual awards is with the use of five-sixteenth inch gold stars (a silver star is used in lieu of five gold stars).

The medal is a bronze compass rose of sixteen points. In the center of the compass is an American eagle swooping down in attack with a lightning bolt in each talon. The medal is suspended from the ribbon by a fleur-de-lis. The back of the medal has a blank raised disk to allow for inscribing the recipient's name. The ribbon is dark blue with orange stripes just inside each edge. A Combat Distinguishing Device "V" was authorized for use with the Air Medal effective 5 April 1974.

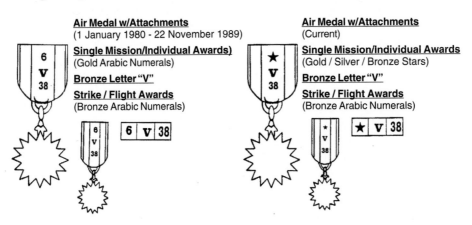

Air Medal w/Attachments
(1 January 1980 - 22 November 1989)

<u>**Single Mission/Individual Awards)**</u>
(Gold Arabic Numerals)

<u>**Bronze Letter "V"**</u>

<u>**Strike / Flight Awards**</u>
(Bronze Arabic Numerals)

Air Medal w/Attachments
(Current)

<u>**Single Mission/Individual Awards**</u>
(Gold / Silver / Bronze Stars)

<u>**Bronze Letter "V"**</u>

<u>**Strike / Flight Awards**</u>
(Bronze Arabic Numerals)

JOINT SERVICE COMMENDATION MEDAL

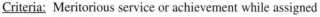

Gold   Silver   Bronze

Instituted: 1963
Criteria: Meritorious service or achievement while assigned
to a Joint Activity
Devices: Bronze letter "V" (for valor), bronze, silver oak leaf cluster

For meritorious achievement or service while assigned to a joint activity. The Joint Service Commendation Medal is worn after the Air Medal and before the Navy and Marine Corps Commendation Medal.

The Joint Service Commendation Medal was established by the Department of Defense on 17 May 1967 and made retroactive to 1 January 1963. The medal is awarded in the name of the Secretary of Defense to members of the Armed Forces who were assigned to the Office of the Secretary of Defense, the Joint Chiefs of Staff, the Defense Agencies or unified commands who have distinguished themselves by outstanding achievement or meritorious service, but to a lesser degree than required for the award of the Defense Meritorious Service Medal.

The Joint Service Commendation Medal was designed by the Army's Institute of Heraldry. The medal consists of four conjoined hexagons of green enamel edged in gold (two vertical and two horizontal). The upper hexagon contains thirteen gold stars and the lower hexagon has a gold heraldic delineation representing land, sea and air. In the center is a gold eagle taken from the Seal of the Department of Defense. The eagle and hexagons are surrounded by a circle of gold laurel leaves with gold bands. The back of the medal has a plaque for inscribing the recipient's name and the raised words FOR MILITARY (above the plaque) and MERIT (below the plaque). The ribbon consists of a green center stripe bordered on each side by stripes of white, green, white and light blue. Additional awards are denoted by oak leaf clusters.

NAVY AND MARINE CORPS COMMENDATION MEDAL

Gold   Silver   Gold

Instituted: 1944/1950
Criteria: Meritorious service or achievement in a combat or noncombat situation based on sustained performance of a superlative nature
Devices: Bronze letter "V" (for valor), gold, silver star
Notes: Originally a ribbon-only award: "Secretary of the Navy Commendation for Achievement Award with Ribbon". Changed to present name in 1994.

For heroic and meritorious achievement or service. The Navy and Marine Corps Commendation is worn after the Joint Service Commendation Medal and before the Joint Service Achievement Medal.

The Navy and Marine Corps Commendation Medal was originally established as a ribbon only award on 11 January 1944. The current medal was authorized by the Secretary of the Navy on 22 March 1950. The medal is awarded for both heroism and meritorious achievement. To be awarded for heroism, the act must be worthy of recognition, but to a lesser degree than required for the Bronze Star Medal in combat or the Navy and Marine Corps Medal in a non-combat situation. To be awarded for meritorious achievement, the act must be outstanding and worthy of special recognition, but to a lesser degree than required for the Bronze Star Medal in combat or the Meritorious Service Medal or Air Medal when in a non-combat situation.

The Navy and Marine Corps Commendation Medal was designed by the Army's Institute of Heraldry. The medal is a bronze hexagon with the eagle from the Seal of the Department of Defense in the center. The back of the medal has a plaque for inscribing the recipients name and the raised words FOR MILITARY (above the plaque) and MERIT (below the plaque). The ribbon is dark green with narrow a stripe of white near each edge. Additional awards of the Navy and Marine Corps Commendation Medal are denoted by five-sixteenth inch gold stars. A Combat Distinguishing Device (Combat "V") may be authorized.

JOINT SERVICE ACHIEVEMENT MEDAL

Silver

Bronze

Instituted: 1983
Criteria: Meritorious service or achievement while serving with a Joint Activity
Devices: Bronze, silver oak leaf cluster

For meritorious service or achievement while assigned to a joint activity after 3 August 1983. The Joint Service Achievement Medal is worn after the Navy and Marine Corps Commendation Medal and before the Navy and Marine Corps Achievement Medal.

The Joint Service Achievement Medal was established by the Department of Defense on 3 August 1983. The medal is awarded in the name of the Secretary of Defense to members of the Armed Forces (below the rank of Colonel) who were assigned to the Office of the Secretary of Defense, the Joint Chiefs of Staff, the Defense Agencies, or unified commands who have distinguished themselves by outstanding achievement or meritorious service, but to a lesser degree than required for the award of the Joint Service Commendation Medal.

The Joint Service Achievement Medal was designed by the Army's Institute of Heraldry. The medal consists of a twelve pointed star with a gold eagle in the center. The eagle is taken from the Seal of the Department of Defense. The reverse of the medal has a circle composed of the raised words JOINT SERVICE ACHIEVEMENT AWARD. The ribbon has a thin red stripe in the center flanked on either side by a wide blue stripe, a thin white stripe, a narrow green stripe, a thin white stripe and a narrow dark blue border. Additional awards are denoted by oak leaf clusters.

NAVY AND MARINE CORPS ACHIEVEMENT MEDAL

Instituted: 1961/1967
Criteria: Meritorious service or achievement in a combat or noncombat situation based on sustained performance of a superlative nature
Devices: Bronze letter "V" (for valor), gold, silver star
Notes: Originally a ribbon-only award: "Secretary of the Navy Commendation for Achievement Award with Ribbon"

Gold   Silver   Gold

For junior officers and enlisted personnel whose professional and/or leadership achievements on or after 1 May 1961 are clearly of a superlative nature. The Navy and Marine Corps Achievement Medal is worn after the Joint Service Achievement Medal and before the Combat Action Ribbon.

The Navy and Marine Corps Achievement Medal was originally established as a ribbon only award on 1 May 1961. The current medal was authorized by the Secretary of the Navy on 17 July 1967. The medal is awarded for both professional and leadership achievement. To be awarded for professional achievement, the act must clearly exceed that which is normally required or expected, and it must be an important contribution to benefit the United States Naval Service. To be recognized for leadership achievement, the act must be noteworthy and contribute to the individual's unit mission.

The Navy and Marine Corps Achievement Medal was designed by the Army's Institute of Heraldry. The medal is a bronze square (with clipped corners) with a fouled anchor in the center. There is a star in each of the four corners. The back of the medal is blank to allow for engraving the recipient's name. The ribbon is myrtle green with stripes of orange near each edge. Additional awards of the Navy and Marine Corps Medal are denoted by five-sixteenth inch gold stars. A Combat Distinguishing Device (Combat "V") may be authorized.

COMBAT ACTION RIBBON

Silver

Gold

<u>Instituted:</u> 1969 - Retroactive to March 1961
<u>Criteria:</u> Active participation in ground or air combat during specifically listed military operations
<u>Devices:</u> Gold, silver star
<u>Notes:</u> This is the only Navyand Marine Corps personal decoration which has no associated medal (a "ribbon-only" award).

For active participation in ground or surface combat subsequent to 1 March 1961, while in the grade of Colonel or below. The Combat Action Ribbon is worn after the Navy and Marine Corps Achievement Medal and before the Navy Presidential Unit Citation in a ribbon display. It is worn as the senior ribbon on the right breast when full-sized medals are worn on the left breast.

The Combat Action Ribbon was authorized by the Secretary of the Navy on 17 February 1969 and made retroactive to 1 March 1961. The principal requirement is that the individual was engaged in combat during which time he/she was under enemy fire and that his/her performance was satisfactory.

The Combat Action Ribbon is a ribbon only award. The ribbon is gold with thin center stripes of red, white and blue and border stripes of dark blue on the left and red on the right. Additional awards are authorized for each separate conflict/war and

NAVY PRESIDENTIAL UNIT CITATION

Silver

Bronze

<u>Instituted:</u> 1942
<u>Criteria:</u> Awarded to Navy/Marine Corps units for extraordinary heroism in action against an armed enemy.
<u>Devices:</u> Bronze, silver star

Awarded in the name of the President for service in a unit with outstanding performance in action. The Navy Presidential Unit Citation is worn after the Combat Action Ribbon and before the Joint Meritorious Unit Award.

The Navy Presidential Unit Citation was established by Executive Order on 6 February 1942 and amended on 28 June 1943. It is awarded by the Secretary of the Navy in the name of the President. The citation is conferred on units for displaying extraordinary heroism subsequent to 16 October 1941. The degree of heroism required is the same as that which is required for the award of the Navy Cross to an individual. An individual assigned to the unit when the award was granted may wear the ribbon as a permanent part of the uniform with a three-sixteenth inch bronze star.

The Navy Presidential Unit Citation is a ribbon only award. The ribbon consists of three equal horizontal stripes of navy blue (top), gold (middle) and red (bottom). Additional awards of the Navy Presidential Unit Citation are denoted by three-sixteenth inch bronze stars.

JOINT MERITORIOUS UNIT AWARD

Silver

Bronze

<u>Instituted:</u> 1981
<u>Criteria:</u> Awarded to Joint Service units for meritorious achievement, or service in combat or extreme circumstances
<u>Devices:</u> Bronze, silver oak leaf cluster

Recognizes joint units or activities for meritorious achievement or service superior to that which is normally expected. The Joint Meritorious Unit Award is worn after the Navy Presidential Unit Citation and before the Navy Unit Commendation.

The Joint Meritorious Unit Award was authorized by the Secretary of Defense on 10 June 1981 and was originally called the Department of Defense Meritorious Unit Award. It is awarded in the name of the Secretary of Defense for meritorious service, superior to that which would normally be expected during combat, or declared national emergency, or under extraordinary circumstances that involve national interest. The service performed by the unit would be similar to that performed by an individual awarded the Defense Superior Service Medal. The award is retroactive to 23 January 1979.

The Joint Meritorious Unit Award is a ribbon only award. The ribbon is similar to the Defense Superior Service Medal ribbon with a gold metal frame with laurel leaves. Like the Defense Superior Service Medal, the ribbon consists of a central stripe of red flanked on either side by stripes of white, blue and yellow with blue edges. Additional awards are denoted by oak leaf clusters.

NAVY UNIT COMMENDATION

Silver

Bronze

Instituted: 1944
Criteria: Awarded to units Navy/Marine Corps for outstanding heroism in action or extremely meritorious service
Devices: Bronze, silver star

For outstanding heroism in action or extremely meritorious service not involving combat, but in support of military operations. The Navy Unit Commendation is worn after the Joint Meritorious Unit Award and before the Navy Meritorious Unit Commendation.

The Navy Unit Commendation was established by the Secretary of the Navy on 18 December 1944. The Commendation is awarded by the Secretary of the Navy with the approval of the President. The Commendation is made to units, which, subsequent to 6 December 1941, distinguish themselves by outstanding heroism in action against an enemy, but to a lesser degree than required for the Presidential Unit Citation. The Commendation may also be awarded for extremely meritorious service not involving combat, but in support of military operations, which is outstanding when compared to other units performing similar service.

The Navy Unit Commendation is a ribbon only award. The ribbon is dark green with narrow border stripes of red, gold and blue. Additional awards are denoted by three-sixteenth inch bronze stars.

NAVY MERITORIOUS UNIT COMMENDATION RIBBON

Silver

Bronze

Instituted: 1967
Criteria: Awarded to Navy/Marine Corps units for valorous actions or meritorious achievement (combat or noncombat)
Devices: Bronze, silver star

For any unit which distinguishes itself by valorous or meritorious achievement or service or outstanding service. The Meritorious Unit Commendation is worn after the Navy Unit Commendation and before the Navy "E" ribbon.

The Navy Meritorious Unit Commendation was established by the Secretary of the Navy on 17 July 1967. The Commendation is awarded by the Secretary of the Navy to units which distinguish themselves by either valorous or meritorious achievement considered outstanding, but to a lesser degree than required for the Navy Unit Commendation. The Commendation may be awarded for services in combat or non-combat situations.

The Navy Meritorious Unit Commendation is a ribbon only award. The ribbon is dark green with a narrow red center stripe flanked on either side by stripes of gold, navy blue and gold. Additional awards are denoted by three-sixteenth inch bronze stars.

NAVY "E" RIBBON

Silver

Silver

Instituted: 1976
Criteria: Awarded to ships or squadrons which have won battle efficiency competitions
Devices: Silver letter "E", wreathed silver letter "E"

To recognize individuals who were permanently assigned to ships or squadrons that won the battle efficiency competitions subsequent to 1 July 1974. The Navy "E" Ribbon is worn after the Meritorious Unit Commendation and before the Prisoner of War Medal on a ribbon display and on the right breast before the Sea Service Deployment Ribbon if wearing full-sized medals.

The Navy "E" Ribbon was established in June 1976 and is authorized to be worn by all personnel who served as permanent members of ship's company or squadrons winning the Battle Efficiency Award.

The Navy "E" Ribbon is a ribbon only award. The ribbon is navy blue with borders of white and gold with a silver "E" in the center. Additional awards are denoted by additional "E"s. The fourth (and final) awards is denoted by an "E" surrounded by a silver wreath.

PRISONER OF WAR MEDAL

Instituted: 1985
Criteria: Awarded to any member of the U.S. Armed Forces taken prisoner during any armed conflict dating from World War I
Devices: Bronze, silver star

Awarded to any person who was taken prisoner of war and held captive after 5 April 1917. The Prisoner of War Medal is worn after the Navy "E" ribbon and before the Good Conduct Medal.

The Prisoner of War Medal was authorized by Public Law Number 99-145 in 1985 and may be awarded to any person who was taken prisoner or held captive while engaged in an action against an enemy of the United States; while engaged in military operations involving conflict with an opposing armed force; or while serving with friendly forces engaged in armed conflict against an opposing armed force in which the United States is not a belligerent party. The recipient's conduct, while a prisoner, must have been honorable.

The Prisoner of War Medal was designed by the Army's Institute of Heraldry. The medal is a circular bronze disc with an American eagle centered and completely surrounded by a ring of barbed wire and bayonet points. The back of the medal has a raised inscription AWARDED TO (with a space for the recipient's name) and FOR HONORABLE SERVICE WHILE A PRISONER OF WAR set in three lines. Below this is the shield of the United States and the words UNITED STATES OF AMERICA. The ribbon is black with thin border stripes of white, blue, white and red. Additional awards are denoted by three-sixteenth inch bronze stars.

MARINE CORPS GOOD CONDUCT MEDAL

Instituted: 1896
Criteria: Outstanding performance and conduct during 3 years of continuous active enlisted service in the U.S Marine Corps
Devices: Bronze, silver star
Notes: Earlier ribbon was 1 1/4" wide

Based on good conduct and faithful service for three year periods of continuous active service. The Marine Corps Good Conduct Medal is worn after the Prisoner of War Medal and before the Selected Marine Corps Reserve Medal.

The Marine Corps Good Conduct Medal was established by the Secretary of the Navy on 20 July 1896. The medal is awarded to an enlisted Marine for obedience, sobriety, military proficiency, neatness, and intelligence during three years of continuous active service. The Marine receiving the award must have had no convictions by court martial and no more than one nonjudicial punishment during the three year period. For the first award the medal may be awarded to the next of kin in those cases where the individual is missing in action or dies of wounds received in combat. A Marine may also receive the medal if separated from the service as a result of wounds incurred in combat.

The Marine Good Conduct Medal was designed by Major General Charles Heywood, the ninth Commandant of the Marine Corps. The medal is a circular bronze disc with an anchor and anchor chain circling an enlisted Marine in the uniform of the late nineteenth century. The Marine is holding the lanyard of a naval rifle (gun) and below this is a scroll with the motto of the Corps SEMPER FIDELIS. In the space between the Marine and the anchor chain is the raised inscription UNITED

Continued on page 72

MARINE CORPS GOOD CONDUCT MEDAL

Continued from page 71

STATES MARINE CORPS. The reverse side of the medal has the raised inscription FIDELITY - ZEAL - OBEDIENCE centered in-between two concentric raised circles and with room in the center to inscribe the recipient's name.

The medal has undergone several design modification since its inception. The original medal incorporated an upper bronze suspension bar bearing the raised inscription U.S. MARINES. Number clasps were used on the original medal to indicate additional awards, which were placed on the suspension ribbon between the upper suspension bar and the medallion. Prior to World War I, medals were engraved with the recipient's name, service number and date span. During World War I, medals were impressed with rim numbers and many were issued without engraving. Following World War II, the Marine Corps changed its practice of engraving to stamping the recipient's information on the medal's reverse. The practice of using a suspension bar and clasps was also eliminated during this period.

The ribbon of the Marine Corps Good Conduct Medal is dark red with a dark blue stripe in the center. The medal is suspended from the ribbon by a bronze rifle pointing to the right. Additional awards are denoted by three-sixteenth bronze stars.

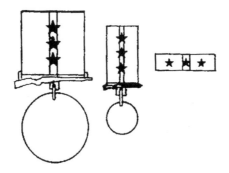

SELECTED MARINE CORPS RESERVE MEDAL

 Silver   Bronze

Instituted: 1939
Criteria: Outstanding performance and conduct during 4 years of service in the Marine Corps Selected Reserve
Devices: Bronze, silver star
Notes: Formerly "Organized Marine Corps Reserve Medal"

Awarded for four consecutive years service in the Selected Marine Corps Reserve. The Selected Marine Corps Reserve Medal is worn after the Good Conduct Medal and before the Marine Corps Expeditionary Medal.

The Selected Marine Corps Reserve Medal was established by the Secretary of the Navy on 19 February 1939 as the Fleet Marine Corps Reserve Medal. Later the name was changed to the Organized Marine Corps Reserve Medal and finally to its current name in the late 1980's. The medal is awarded to members of the Marine Corps Reserve who, subsequent to 1 July 1925, and prior to 24 April 1961, attended 80 percent of all scheduled drills during a four year period. Since 24 April 1961 the attendance criteria was raised to 90 percent.

The Selected Marine Corps Reserve Medal was designed by the United States Mint. The medal is a circular bronze disc with two walking figures. The figure in the foreground is wearing a pre-World War II uniform, and the other is wearing civilian clothes. Above the figures is the raised circular inscription MARINE CORPS RESERVE and below the figures is the inscription FOR SERVICE. The back of the medal is identical to the back of the Marine Corps Good Conduct Medal with the raised inscription FIDELITY - ZEAL - OBEDIENCE centered in-between two concentric raised circles and with room in the center to inscribe the recipients name. The ribbon is gold with a red center stripe with narrow border stripes of blue, white and red. Additional awards are denoted by three-sixteenth bronze stars.

MARINE CORPS EXPEDITIONARY MEDAL

Silver   Silver   Bronze

Instituted: 1919/1921
Dates: 1919 to present
Criteria: Landings on foreign territory and operations against armed opposition for which no specific campaign medal has been authorized
Devices: Silver letter "W", bronze, silver star
Notes: Originally a "ribbon-only" award
Bar: "Wake Island"

WAKE ISLAND

For opposed landing on a foreign territory or operations deserving special recognition. The Marine Corps Expeditionary Medal is worn after the Selected Marine Corps Reserve Medal and before the China Service Medal.

The Marine Corps Expeditionary Ribbon was authorized by Marine Corps General Order on 8 May 1919. The medal pendant was added on 28 July 1921 by Executive Order 3524. The medal is awarded to members of the Marine Corps who have engaged in operations against armed opposition in foreign territory, or have served in situations warranting special recognition where no other campaign medal was awarded. To date more than sixty operations have qualified for the award, the latest being operations in the Persian Gulf prior to Desert Shield/Desert Storm.

The Marine Corps Expeditionary Medal was designed by Walter Hancock. The medal is a circular bronze disc showing a Marine charging from the sea (depicted by wave scrolls at his feet). The Marine is in a uniform of the post World War I period with a full pack and fixed bayonet. Above, in a semicircle, is a raised inscription EXPEDITIONS. The reverse of the medal shows an American eagle perched on an anchor and laurel branches. On either side of the eagle are the words FOR SERVICE. Above, in a semicircle is a raised inscription UNITED STATES MARINE CORPS. The ribbon is cardinal red and gold, the official colors of the Corps. The ribbon has a wide red center stripe flanked by gold (sometimes mistaken for khaki) with narrow red edges. Additional awards are denoted by three-sixteenth inch bronze stars. For those who served in defense of Wake Island there is a one-quarter inch silver "W" for the ribbon bar and a clasp for the medal inscribed WAKE ISLAND.

CHINA SERVICE MEDAL

Bronze

Instituted: 1940
Dates: 1937-39, 1945-57
Criteria: Service ashore in China or on-board naval vessels during either of the above periods
Devices: Bronze star
Notes: Medal was reinstituted in 1947 for extended service during dates shown above

For service in China during the periods just prior to and just following World War II. The China Service Medal is worn after the Marine Corps Expeditionary Medal and before the American Defense Service Medal.

The China Service Medal was authorized by the Department of the Navy on 23 August 1940 for members of the Navy and Marine Corps who served in China or were attached to ships in the area during the period 7 July 1937 to 7 September 1939. The second period was for those who were present for duty during operations in China, Taiwan, and the Matsu Straits during the period 2 September 1947 to 1 April 1957.

The China Service Medal was designed by George Snowden. The medal is a circular bronze disc showing a Chinese junk under full sail with the raised inscribed words CHINA above and SERVICE below. The reverse of the medal shows an American eagle perched on an anchor and laurel branches. On either side of the eagle are the words FOR SERVICE. Above, in a semicircle is a raised inscription UNITED STATES MARINE CORPS. The ribbon is yellow with a narrow red stripe near each edge. If an individual served during both periods, a bronze three-sixteenth inch star is worn.

AMERICAN DEFENSE SERVICE MEDAL

 Bronze **A** Bronze

Instituted: 1941
Dates: 1939-41
Criteria: For active duty during national and limited emergencies just prior to World War II
Devices: Bronze star (denotes bars below); bronze letter "A" (not worn with bronze star)
Bars: : "Base" and "Fleet"

 FLEET    BASE

    For service during periods of national and limited emergencies just prior to World War II. The American Defense Service Medal is worn after the China Service Medal and before the American Campaign Medal.

    The American Defense Service Medal was established by Executive Order on 28 June 1941. The Department of the Navy authorized the medal for the Navy and Marine Corps on 20 April 1942. The medal was awarded to members of the Armed Forces for service during the period of 8 September 1939 to 7 December 1941.

    The American Defense Service Medal was designed by Lee Lawrie. The medal is a circular bronze disc with a female figure (Liberty) brandishing a sword and holding a shield. The figure is standing on an oak branch with four leaves representing four services. Above are the inscribed words AMERICAN DEFENSE. The reverse has the raised inscription FOR SERVICE DURING THE LIMITED EMERGENCY PROCLAIMED BY THE PRESIDENT ON 8 SEPTEMBER 1939 OR DURING THE LIMITED EMERGENCY PROCLAIMED BY THE PRESIDENT ON 27 MAY 1941 set in twelve lines. Below this is a spray of seven oak leaves. The ribbon is yellow with narrow red, white and blue stripes near each edge. The Navy and Marine Corps had two clasps for the medal. The FLEET clasp was awarded for service with the fleet on the high seas and the BASE clasp was for service at bases outside the United States. A three-sixteenth inch bronze star was worn on the ribbon bar to denote the award of a clasp. In addition to the clasps, the block letter "A" was authorized for wear on the ribbon bar and medal suspension ribbon by personnel who served in the Atlantic Fleet on the high seas prior to the outbreak of World War II.

AMERICAN CAMPAIGN MEDAL

 Bronze

Instituted: 1942
Dates: 1941-46
Criteria: Service outside the U.S. in the American theater for 30 days, or within the continental U.S. for one year.
Devices: Bronze star

    For service during World War II within the American Theater of Operations. The American Campaign Medal is worn after the American Defense Service Medal and before the European - African - Middle Eastern Campaign Medal.

    The American Campaign Medal was established by Executive Order on 6 November 1942 and amended on 15 March 1946, which established a closing date. The medal is awarded to all members of the Armed Forces who served in the American Theater of Operations during the period from 7 December 1941 to 2 March 1946, or was awarded a combat decoration while in combat against the enemy. The service must have been an aggregate of one year within the continental United States, or thirty consecutive days outside the continental United States, or sixty nonconsecutive days outside the continental United States, but within the American Theater of Operations. Maps of the three theaters of operations during World War II were drawn on 6 November 1942 to include the American Theater, the European - African - Middle Eastern Theater and the Asiatic - Pacific Theater.

    The American Campaign Medal was designed by the Army's Institute of Heraldry. The medal is a circular bronze disc showing a Navy cruiser, a B-24 bomber and a sinking enemy submarine above three waves. Shown in the background are some buildings representing the United States. Above is the raised inscription AMERICAN CAMPAIGN. The reverse of the medal shows an American eagle standing on a rock. On the left of the eagle are the raised inscribed dates 1941 - 1945 and on the right UNITED STATES OF AMERICA. The ribbon is azure blue with three narrow stripes of red, white and blue (United States) in the center, and four stripes of white, red (Japan), black and white (Germany) near the edges. Three-sixteenth inch bronze stars indicated participation in specialized anti-submarine, escort or special operations.

EUROPEAN-AFRICAN-MIDDLE EASTERN CAMPAIGN MEDAL

Silver

Bronze

Instituted: 1942
Dates: 1941-45
Criteria: Service in the European-African-Middle Eastern theater for 30 days or receipt of any combat decoration
Devices: Bronze, silver star

For service during World War II within the European, African, Middle Eastern Theater of Operations. The European - African - Middle Eastern Campaign Medal is worn after the American Campaign Medal and before the Asiatic - Pacific Campaign Medal.

The European - African - Middle Eastern Campaign Medal was established by Executive Order on 6 November 1942 and amended on 15 March 1946, which established a closing date. The medal is awarded to all members of the Armed Forces who served in the European, African, Middle Eastern Theater of Operations during the period from 7 December 1941 to 2 March 1946. The service must have been as a member of the Armed Forces on permanent assignment in the theater, or within the theater on temporary assignment for thirty consecutive days, or sixty nonconsecutive days, or the award of a combat decoration in the theater. Maps of the three theaters of operations during World War II were drawn on 6 November, 1942 to include the American Theater, the European - African - Middle Eastern Theater and the Asiatic - Pacific Theater.

The European - African - Middle Eastern Campaign Medal was designed by the Army's Institute of Heraldry. The medal is a circular bronze disc showing troops assaulting a beach. A LST (Landing Ship Tank) and an airplane are in the background. Above is the raised inscription EUROPEAN AFRICAN MIDDLE EASTERN CAMPAIGN set in three lines. The reverse of the medal shows an American eagle standing on a rock. On the left of the eagle are the raised inscribed dates 1941 - 1945 and on the right UNITED STATES OF AMERICA. The ribbon has narrow center stripes of red, white and blue (United States). These are flanked by wide stripes of green on the left by narrow stripes of green, white and red (Italy), and on the right by narrow stripes of white, black and white (Germany). The stripes at the edges are brown (Africa). Participation in specific combat operations is denoted by three-sixteenth inch bronze stars. A three-sixteenth inch silver star is worn in lieu of five bronze stars.

The nine Marine Corps campaign designations for the European - African Middle Eastern Campaign Medal are:

North African Occupation,
8 November 1942 - 9 July 1943

Northwest Greenland Operation,
10 June - 17 November 1944

Sicilian Occupation,
9 - 15 July and 28 July - 17 August 1943

Invasion of Southern France,
15 August - 25 September 1944

Salarno Landings,
9 - 12 September 1943

Reinforcement of Malta,
14 - 21 April and 3 - 16 May 1942

West Coast of Italy Operations,
22 January - 17 June 1944

Russian Convoy Operations,
16 December 1941 - 27 February 1943

Invasion of Normandy,
6 - 25 June 1944

ASIATIC - PACIFIC CAMPAIGN MEDAL

Silver

Bronze

Instituted: 1942
Dates: 1941-46
Criteria: Service in the Asiatic-Pacific theater for 30 day or receipt of any combat decoration
Devices: Bronze, silver star; bronze arrowhead

For service during World War II within the Asiatic Pacific Theater of Operations. The Asiatic - Pacific Campaign Medal is worn after the European - African - Middle Eastern Campaign Medal and before the World War II Victory Medal.

The Asiatic - Pacific Campaign Medal was established by Executive Order on 6 November 1942 and amended on 15 March 1946, which established a closing date. The medal is awarded to all members of the Armed Forces who served in the Asiatic Pacific Theater of Operations during the period from 7 December 1941 to 2 March 1946. The service must have been as a member of the Armed Forces on permanent assignment in the theater, or within the theater on temporary assignment for thirty consecutive days, or sixty nonconsecutive days, the award of a combat decoration in the theater. Maps of the three theaters of operations during World War II were drawn on 6 November 1942 to include the American Theater, the European - African - Middle Eastern Theater and the Asiatic - Pacific Theater.

The Asiatic - Pacific Campaign Medal was designed by the Army's Institute of Heraldry. The medal is a circular bronze disc showing troops landing in a tropical setting with a palm tree, battleship, aircraft carrier and submarine in the background. At the top of the medal, around the edge, are the words ASIATIC PACIFIC CAMPAIGN. The reverse of the medal shows an American eagle standing on a rock. On the left of the eagle are the raised inscribed dates 1941 - 1945 and on the right UNITED STATES OF AMERICA. The ribbon is yellow-orange with narrow center stripes of red, white and blue (United States). Near the edges are narrow white, red and white stripes (Japan). Participation in specific combat operations is denoted by three-sixteenth inch bronze stars. A three-sixteenth inch silver star is worn in lieu of five bronze stars.

The forty-two Marine Corps campaign designations for the Asiatic - Pacific Campaign Medal are:

Pearl Harbor-Midway, 1941
Wake Island, 1941
Philippine Islands Operation, 1941-1942
Netherlands East Indies, 1941-1942
Pacific Raids, 1942
Coral Sea, 1942
Midway, 1942
Guadalcanal,-Tulagi Landings, 1942
Capture and Defense of Guadalcanal, 1942-1943
Makin Raid, 1942
Eastern Solomons (Stewart Isl.), 1942
Buin-Faisi-Tonolai, 1942
Cape Esperance (Second Savo), 1942
Santa Cruz Islands, 1942
Guadalcanal (Third Savo), 1942
Tassafaronga (Fourth Savo), 1942
Eastern New Guinea, 1942-1944
Rennel Island Operation, 1943
Solomon Islands Consolidation, 1943-1945
Aleutians Operations, 1943
New Georgia Group Operation, 1943

Bismarck Archipelago, 1943-1944
Pacific Raids, 1943
Treasury-Bougainville Operation, 1943
Gilbert Island Operation, 1943
Marshall Islands Operation, 1943-1944
Asiatic-Pacific Raids, 1944
Western New Guinea, 1944-1945
Hollandia Operation, 1944
Marianas Operation
Capture and Occupation of Tinian, 1944
Western Caroline Islands, 1944
Leyte Operation, 1944
Luzon Operation, 1944-1945
Iwo Jima Operation, 1945
Okinawa Gunto Operation, 1945
Third Fleet Operations against Japan, 1945
Kurile Islands Operation, 1944-1945
Borneo Operation, 1945
Consolidation of Southern Philippines, 1945
Manila Bay-Bicol Operation, 1945
Naval Group China, 1943-1945

WORLD WAR II VICTORY MEDAL

Instituted: 1945
Dates: 1941-46
Criteria: Awarded for service in the U.S. Armed Forces during the above period
Devices: None

For service during World War II. The World War II Victory Medal is worn after the Asiatic-Pacific Campaign Medal and before the Navy Occupation Service Medal.

The World War II Victory Medal was authorized on 6 July 1945. The medal was awarded to all members of the Armed Forces who served on active duty during the period from 7 December 1941 to 31 December 1946. It was also awarded to members of the Philippine Armed Forces.

The World War II Victory Medal was designed by the Army's Institute of Heraldry. The medal is a circular bronze disc showing the figure of Liberty holding the hilt of a broken sword in her right hand and the broken blade in her left; her right foot is resting on an ancient war helmet. Also at the figure's feet, behind the helmet, is a sun with rays spreading upward. The figure separates the raised inscription WORLD WAR II. The reverse of the medal has raised inscriptions FREEDOM FROM FEAR AND WANT and FREEDOM OF SPEECH AND RELIGION, separated by a palm branch. Around the edge of the reverse are the inscribed words UNITED STATES OF AMERICA and the dates 1941 - 1945. The ribbon has a wide dark red center stripe bordered by narrow stripes of white. The borders consist of bands of color starting in the center with red flanked by orange, yellow, green, blue and navy. No attachments are authorized for the World War II Victory Medal, although some veterans state that they received the medal with a three-sixteenth inch bronze star affixed. They believe that the star was to distinguish them as having been overseas at the end of the war. Although this may have been the practice, I have found no documentation to support the attachment.

NAVY OCCUPATION SERVICE MEDAL

 Gold Airplane

Instituted: 1948
Dates: 1945-55 (Berlin: 1945-90)
Criteria: 30 consecutive days of service in occupied territories of former enemies during above period
Devices: Gold airplane
Bars: "Europe", "Asia"

EUROPE	ASIA

For thirty consecutive days of service in occupied zones following World War II. The Navy Occupation Service Medal is worn after the World War II Victory Medal and before the Medal for Humane Action.

The Navy Occupation Service Medal was authorized by ALNAV 24 on 22 January 1947 and Navy Department GO on 28 January 1948. The medal was awarded for occupation duty in Japan and Korea from 2 September 1945 to 27 April 1952. The medal was also awarded for occupation service in Germany, Italy, Trieste and Austria.

The Navy Occupation Service Medal was designed by the Army's Institute of Heraldry. The medal is a circular bronze disc showing Neptune, god of the sea, riding a sea serpent with the head and front legs of a horse. Neptune is holding a trident in his right hand and pointing to an image of land, at the left of the medal, with his left hand. The lower front of the medal depicts the ocean with the words OCCUPATION SERVICE in two lines. The reverse of the medal shows an American eagle perched on an anchor and laurel branches. On either side of the eagle are the words FOR SERVICE. Above, in a semicircle is a raised inscription UNITED STATES MARINE CORPS. The ribbon has two wide stripes of red and black in the center with border stripes of white. Clasps, similar to those used on the World War I Victory Medal, are used to denote service in "EUROPE" and "ASIA", which are authorized for wear with the medal. There are no devices authorized for wear on the ribbon bar which represents these clasps. In addition, Navy and Marine personnel who served 90 consecutive days in support of the Berlin Airlift (1948-1949) are authorized to wear the Berlin Airlift device, a three-eighths inch gold C-54 airplane, on the ribbon bar and suspension ribbon.

MEDAL FOR HUMANE ACTION

Instituted: 1949
Dates: 1948-49
Criteria: 120 consecutive days of service participating in the Berlin Airlift or in support thereof
Devices: None

For service in support of the Berlin Airlift. The Medal for Humane Action is worn after the Navy Occupation Service Medal and before the National Defense Service Medal.

The Medal for Humane Action was authorized by Congress on 20 July 1949 for service of at least 120 days while participating in , or providing direct support for, the Berlin Airlift. The airlift period was from 26 June 1948 to 30 September, 1949.

The Medal for Humane Action was designed by the Army's Institute of Heraldry. The medal is a circular bronze disc with a depiction of a C-54 aircraft, which carried the majority of the airlift. The C-54 is centered on the medal above the Berlin coat of arms, which lies in the center of a wreath of wheat. The reverse has the American eagle, from the seal of the Department of Defense, above the raised inscription TO SUPPLY NECESSITIES OF LIFE TO THE PEOPLE OF BERLIN GERMANY. The words FOR HUMANE ACTION appear arched above the eagle. The ribbon is medium blue with borders of black edged (inboard) by narrow white stripes. In the center are narrow stripes of white, red and white. No attachments are authorized for this medal.

NATIONAL DEFENSE SERVICE MEDAL

Bronze

Instituted: 1953
Dates: 1950-54, 1961-74, 1990-95
Criteria: Any honorable active duty service during any of the above periods
Devices: Bronze star
Notes: Reinstituted in 1966 and 1991 for Vietnam and Southwest Asia (Gulf War) actions respectively

For active federal service in the Armed Forces during the periods 1950-54, 1961-74 and 1990-95. The National Defense Service Medal is worn after the Medal for Humane Action and before the Korean Service Medal.

The National Defense Service Medal was authorized by Executive Order on 22 April 1953. The medal was awarded for active service during the Korean War (27 June 1950 to 27 July 1954), the Vietnam War (1 January 1961 to 14 August 1974) and Desert Shield/Desert Storm (2 August 1990 to 30 November 1995).

The National Defense Service Medal was designed by the Army's Institute of Heraldry. The medal is a circular bronze disc with the American bald eagle perched on a sword and palm branch. Above the eagle, in a semicircle, are the raised engraved words NATIONAL DEFENSE. The reverse shows a shield from the Great Seal of the United States with an oak and laurel leave spray in a semicircle below it. The ribbon is red with a wide center stripe of yellow bordered by thin stripes of red, white, blue and white. Three-sixteenth inch bronze stars are used to denote each additional period of qualifying service.

KOREAN SERVICE MEDAL

Silver

Bronze

Instituted: 1950
Dates: 1950-54
Criteria: Participation in military operations within the Korean area during the above period
Devices: Bronze, silver star

For participation in operations in the Korean area during the Korean Conflict. The Korean Service Medal is worn after the National Defense Service Medal and before the Antarctica Service Medal.

The Korean Service Medal was authorized by Executive Order on 8 November 1950. The medal was awarded to members of the Armed Forces for service in Korea from 27 June 1950 to 27 July 1954. The service required was one or more days in the designated area while attached to or serving with an organization or on a naval vessel that was participating in combat operations or in direct support of combat missions. Thirty consecutive days or sixty nonconsecutive days were required for individuals on Temporary Additional Duty unless the personnel participated in actual combat, in which case the time period was waived.

The Korean Service Medal was designed by the Army's Institute of Heraldry. The medal is a circular bronze disc showing a Korean gateway encircled by a raised inscription KOREAN SERVICE. The reverse of the medal shows the symbol from the Korean national flag representing the unity of all being. Around this symbol is the raised inscription UNITED STATES OF AMERICA with an oak and laurel spray at the bottom. The ribbon is light blue with a thin white stripe in the center and narrow white stripes at the edges. There were ten separate operations during the Conflict, service in each of which entitled the recipient to one three-sixteenth inch bronze star or a three-sixteenth inch silver star in lieu of five bronze stars.

The ten Navy and Marine Corps campaign designations for the Korean Service Medal are:

North Korean aggression,
27 June 1950 - 2 November 1950

Communist China aggression,
3 November 1950 - 24 January 1951

Inchon Landing,
13 September - 17 September 1950

1st United Nations counteroffensive,
25 January 1951 - 21 April 1951

Communist China spring offensive,
22 April 1951 - 8 July 1951

United Nations summer-fall offensive,
9 July 1951 - 27 November 1951

2nd Korean winter,
28 November 1951 - 30 April 1952

Korean defensive, summer-fall 1952,
1 May 1952 - 30 November 1952

3rd Korean winter,
1 December 1952 - 30 April 1953

Korean summer 1953,
1 May 1953 - 27 July 1953

ANTARCTICA SERVICE MEDAL

Bronze, Gold, or Silver

Instituted: 1960
Dates: 1946 to Present
Criteria: 30 calendar days of service on the Antarctic Continent
Devices: Bronze, gold, silver disks
Bars: "Wintered Over" in bronze, gold, silver

WINTERED OVER

For participation in an expedition, operation or support of a U.S. operation in Antarctica after 1 January 1946. The Antarctica Service Medal is worn after the Korean Service Medal and before the Armed Forces Expeditionary Medal.

The Antarctica Service Medal was established by an Act of Congress on 7 July 1960. The ribbon was approved in 1961 and the medal in 1963. The medal is awarded to any American or resident alien who subsequent to 1 January 1946, served on the Antarctic continent on or in support of U.S. operations there. Originally no minimum time was required for the medal; since 1 June 1973 a minimum of 30 consecutive days at sea or ashore south of sixty degrees latitude is required. One day on the continent count for two days toward the thirty day eligibility.

The Antarctica Service Medal was designed by the U.S. Mint. The medal is a circular green-gold disc showing a man in the center with Antarctic clothing. On either side of the man is the raised inscription ANTARCTICA SERVICE. In the distant background is a mountain range and a line of clouds. The medal's reverse has the words COURAGE, SACRIFICE and DEVOTION set in the lines over a polar projection of the Antarctic continent. Around the edges is a border of penguins and marine life. The ribbon has a narrow white center stripe flanked on either side by progressively darker shades of blue and borders of black. Individuals who spend the months of March to October are entitled to wear a bronze clasp with the words WINTERED OVER on the suspension ribbon for the first stay, a gold clasp for the second stay and a silver clasp representing a third winter on the Antarctic continent. Five-sixteenth inch discs of the same finish are worn on the ribbon bar to represent the clasps.

THE ARMED FORCES EXPEDITIONARY MEDAL

Silver

Bronze

Instituted: 1961
Dates: 1958 to Present
Criteria: Participation in military operations not covered by a specific campaign medal
Devices: Bronze, silver star
Notes: Authorized for service in Vietnam until establishment of Vietnam Service Medal

For participating in designated operations after 1 July 1958. The Armed Forces Expeditionary Medal is worn after the Antarctica Service Medal and before the Vietnam Service Medal.

The Armed Forces Expeditionary Medal was established by Executive Order on 4 December 1961. The medal is awarded to any member of the Armed Forces who participates in or is in support of U. S. Military operations, U.S. Military operations in support of the United Nations, or U.S. Military operations of assistance to friendly nations for which a specific campaign medal has not been established. A minimum of thirty consecutive days, or sixty nonconsecutive days are required for eligibility, unless the period of the operation was less than thirty days and in that case full participation during the operation is required. Additionally, personnel engaged in combat, or an equally hazardous duty, qualify for the award without regard to time in the area. The medal was initially awarded for Vietnam service between 1 July 1958 and 3 July 1965, prior to the establishment of the Vietnam Service Medal. An individual awarded this medal for this period of Vietnam service may either keep the medal or request the Vietnam Service Medal, but may not have both for this service.

The Armed Forces Expeditionary Medal was designed by the Army's Institute of Heraldry. The medal is a circular bronze disc with an American eagle, with wings raised, perched on a sword in front of a compass rose. The design is encircled by the words ARMED FORCES at the top and EXPEDITIONARY SERVICE at the bottom. These words are separated by sprigs of laurel. The reverse of the medal has the shield which appears on the Presidential seal, encircled with branches of laurel at the bottom and the raised inscription UNITED STATES OF AMERICA at the top. The ribbon is light blue with three narrow stripes of red, white and blue in the center and borders of black, brown, yellow and green. Three-sixteenth inch bronze stars are authorized for the current twenty-four qualifying operations. A three-sixteenth inch silver star is worn in lieu of five bronze stars.

To date the Armed Forces Expeditionary Medal has been awarded for the following operations:

Lebanon, 1958
Taiwan Straights, 1958 - 1959
Quemoy & Matsu Islands, 1958 - 1963
Vietnam, 1958 - 1965
Congo, 1960 - 1962
Laos, 1961 - 1962
Berlin, 1961 - 1963
Cuba, 1962 - 1963
Congo, 1964
Dominican Republic, 1965 - 1966
Korea, 1966 - 1974
Cambodia, Thailand, 1973

Cambodia Evacuation, 1975
Mayaquez Operation, 1975
Vietnam Evacuation, 1975
El Salvador, 1981 - 1992
Grenada, 1983
Lebanon, 1983 - 1987
Libia, 1986
Persian Gulf, 1987 - 1990
Panama, 1989 - 1990
Somalia, 1992 - 1995
Haiti, 1994 - 1995
Iraq/Persion Gulf, 1995 - TBD

VIETNAM SERVICE MEDAL

Silver

Bronze

<u>Instituted:</u> 1965
<u>Dates:</u> 1965-73
<u>Criteria:</u> Service in Vietnam, Laos, Cambodia or Thailand during the above period
<u>Devices:</u> Bronze, silver star

For service in Southeast Asia and contiguous waters or airspace during the Vietnam War. The Vietnam Service Medal is worn after the Armed Forces Expeditionary Medal and before the Southwest Asia Service Medal.

The Vietnam Service Medal was established by Executive Order on 8 July 1965. The medal was awarded to all members of the Armed Forces who served in Vietnam and contiguous waters and airspace from 3 July 1965 to 28 March 1973. In addition individuals serving in Laos, Thailand, or Cambodia in direct support of operations in Vietnam during the same period are also eligible Individuals previously awarded the Armed Forces Expeditionary Medal for service in Vietnam between July 1958 and July 1965 may, upon request, exchange that medal for the Vietnam Service Medal.

The Vietnam Service Medal was designed by Thomas Jones, formerly a sculptor with the Army's Institute of Heraldry. The medal is a circular bronze disc with a dragon behind a grove of bamboo trees. Below the design is the three line raised inscription REPUBLIC OF VIETNAM SERVICE. The reverse of the medal shows a crossbow below a torch with the raised inscription UNITED STATES OF AMERICA encircling the lower edge. The ribbon is yellow with three narrow red stripes in the center and narrow green stripes at the borders. Three-sixteenth bronze stars denote participation in each one of the seventeen Vietnam campaigns with a three-sixteenth inch silver star worn in lieu of five bronze stars.

The seventeen Navy and Marine Corps campaign designations for the Vietnam Service Medal are:

Vietnam Advisory Campaign,
15 March 1962 - 7 March 1965

Vietnam Defense Campaign,
8 March 1965 - 24 December 1965

Vietnam Counteroffensive,
25 December 1965 - 30 June 1966

Vietnam Counteroffensive Phase II,
1 July 1966 - 31 May 1967

Vietnam Counteroffensive Phase III,
1 June 1967 - 29 January 1968

TET Counteroffensive,
30 January 1968 - 1 April 1968

Vietnam Counteroffensive Phase IV,
2 April 1968 - 30 June 1968

Vietnam Counteroffensive Phase V,
1 July 1968 - 1 November 1968

Vietnam Counteroffensive Phase VI,
2 November 1968 - 22 February 1969

TET '69 Counteroffensive,
23 February 1969 - 8 June 1969

Vietnam Summer -Fall 1969,
9 June 1969 - 31 October 1969

Vietnam Winter - Spring 1970,
1 November 1969 - 30 April 1970

Sanctuary Counteroffensive,
1 May 1970 - 30 June 1970

Vietnam Counteroffensive Phase VII,
1 July 1970 - 30 June 1971

Consolidation I,
1 July 1971 - 30 November 1971

Consolidation II,
1 December 1971 - 29 March 1972

Vietnam Cease-fire Campaign,
30 March 1972 - 28 January 1973

SOUTHWEST ASIA SERVICE MEDAL

Bronze

<u>Instituted:</u> 1991
<u>Dates:</u> 1990-1995
<u>Criteria:</u> Active participation in, or support of, Operations Desert Shield and/or Desert Storm
<u>Devices:</u> Bronze star
<u>Notes:</u> Terminal date of service was 30 November 1995

For service in Southwest Asia during Desert Shield/Desert Storm operations, or what is often referred to as the Persian Gulf War. The Southwest Asia Service Medal is worn after the Vietnam Service Medal and before the Armed Forces Service Medal.

The Southwest Asia Service Medal was established by Executive Order on 12 March 1991. The medal is awarded to all members of the Armed Forces who participated in military operations, or in direct support of military operations in Southwest Asia and contiguous waters and airspace from 2 August 1990 to 30 November 1995.

The Southwest Asia Service Medal was designed by the Army's Institute of Heraldry. The medal is a circular bronze disc with the upper part of the medal showing a desert setting with a rising sun, tent, troops, armored personnel carrier and helicopter. The lower portion of the medal shows a sea setting with clouds, a warship and two fixed wing aircraft. The two settings are separated by the raised inscription SOUTHWEST ASIA SERVICE set in two lines. The reverse of the medal has a sword entwined with a palm leaf pointing up encircled by the raised inscription UNITED STATES OF AMERICA. The ribbon is tan with black borders and a thin black stripe in the center flanked on either side by stripes of green. Between the center stripes and the borders are narrow stripes of red, white and blue. One three-sixteenth bronze star is worn for participation in one of three campaigns.

The three Navy and Marine Corps campaign designations for the Southwest Asia Service Medal are:

Defense of Saudi Arabia,
2 August 1990 - 16 January 1991

Liberation and Defense of Kuwait,
17 January 1991 - 11 April 1991

Cease-fire,
12 April 1995 - 30 November 1995

ARMED FORCES SERVICE MEDAL

Silver

Bronze

Instituted: 1996
Dates: 1992 to Present
Criteria: Participation in military operations not covered by a specific war medal or the Armed Forces Expeditionary Medal
Devices: Bronze, silver star

    For participating in peaceful military operations deemed significant on, or after 1 June 1992. The Armed Forces Service Medal is worn after the Southwest Asia Service Medal and before the Humanitarian Service Medal.

    The Armed Forces Service Medal was authorized by Executive Order on 11 January 1996. The medal is awarded to any member of the Armed Forces who participates in a military operation deemed to be a significant activity in which no foreign armed opposition or hostile action is encountered and for which no other U.S. service medal is authorized. Qualification includes at least one day of participation in the designated area. Direct support of the operation and aircraft flights within the area also qualify for this award as long as at least one day is served within the designated area.

    The Armed Forces Service Medal was designed by the Army's Institute of Heraldry. The medal is a circular bronze disc which displays the torch from the Statue of Liberty in the center encircled by the raised inscription ARMED FORCES SERVICE MEDAL. The reverse of the medal shows the eagle from the Seal of the Department of Defense encircled by a laurel wreath and the raised inscription IN PURSUIT OF DEMOCRACY. The ribbon has a wide light blue center stripe flanked by narrow stripes of tan, olive green and dark green. The borders are narrow stripes of tan. Three-sixteenth inch bronze stars denote successive awards of this medal.

HUMANITARIAN SERVICE MEDAL

Silver

Bronze

Instituted: 1977
Dates: 1975 to Present
Criteria: Direct participation in specific operations of a humanitarian nature
Devices: Bronze, silver star

    For meritorious direct participation in military operations not covered a specific war medal. The Humanitarian Service Medal is worn after the Armed Forces Service Medal and before the Outstanding Volunteer Service Medal.

    The Humanitarian Service Medal was authorized by Executive Order on 19 January 1977. The medal was established to honor members of the Armed Forces who distinguish themselves by meritorious direct participation in a significant military operation of a humanitarian nature, or rendered a service to mankind. The participation must be "hands on" at the site of the operation. Recent qualifying operations include the Oklahoma City Bombing Disaster Relief Operation (19 April - 3 May 1995) and Southeast Flood Disaster Relief Operation (July - August 1994).

    The Humanitarian Service Medal was designed by the Army's Institute of Heraldry. The medal is a circular bronze disc which displays a right hand open and pointing upward within a circle. At the top of the medal's reverse is the raised inscription FOR HUMANITARIAN SERVICE set in three lines. In the center is an oak branch with three acorns and leaves and below this, around the edge, is the raised inscription UNITED STATES ARMED FORCES. The ribbon is medium blue with a wide center stripe of navy blue. The ribbon is edged by a wide stripe of purple with a narrow stripe of white inboard. Additional awards are denoted by three-sixteenth inch bronze stars.

OUTSTANDING VOLUNTEER SERVICE MEDAL

Silver

Bronze

Instituted: 1993
Dates: 1993 to Present
Criteria: Awarded for outstanding and sustained voluntary service
to the civilian community
Devices: Bronze, silver star

    For outstanding and sustained voluntary service to a civilian community. The Outstanding Volunteer Service Medal is worn after the Humanitarian Service Medal and before the Armed Forces Reserve Medal when medals are worn and before the Navy Sea Service Deployment Ribbon on a ribbon display.

    The Outstanding Volunteer Service Medal was established by Executive Order on 9 January 1993. The medal is intended to recognize members of the Armed Forces who perform outstanding volunteer service to a civilian community. The service performed must be strictly voluntary and not duty-related and must reflect sustained direct individual involvement in the volunteer activity (the medal is not intended to recognize a single act). Both Active Duty and Reserve personnel are eligible.

    The Outstanding Volunteer Service Medal was designed by the Army's Institute of Heraldry. The medal is a circular bronze disc with a five pointed star in the center. The star has rings around each point and is encircled with a stylized laurel wreath. The reverse of the medal has an oak leaf branch with three oak leaves and two acorns and the raised inscription OUTSTANDING VOLUNTEER SERVICE set in three lines. Around the bottom edge are the words UNITED STATES OF AMERICA. The ribbon is medium blue with two yellow stripes in the center, each bordered with thin green stripes. Additional orange stripes (not bordered) are near the edges. Additional awards are denoted by three-sixteenth inch bronze stars.

NAVY SEA SERVICE DEPLOYMENT RIBBON

Silver

Bronze

Instituted: 1981
Dates: Retroactive to 1974
Criteria: 12 months active duty on deployed vessels operating away from their
home port for extended periods
Devices: Bronze, silver star

    To recognize the unique and demanding nature of sea service and the arduous duty attendant with deployment. The Navy Sea Service Deployment Ribbon is worn after the Outstanding Volunteer Service Medal and before the Navy Arctic Service Ribbon.

    The Navy Sea Service Deployment Ribbon was approved by the Secretary of the Navy in 1981 and made retroactive to 15 August 1974. The ribbon was created to recognize the unique and demanding nature of sea service and the arduous duty attendant with such service deployments. The award is made to Navy and Marine Corps personnel for twelve months of accumulated sea duty or duty with the Fleet Marine Force, which includes at least one ninety day deployment.

    The Navy Sea Service Deployment Ribbon is a ribbon only award. The ribbon consists of a wide center stripe of light blue, bordered on either side by a narrow stripe of medium blue and equal stripes of gold, red and navy blue. Additional awards are denoted by three-sixteenth inch bronze stars.

NAVY ARCTIC SERVICE RIBBON

Instituted: 1986
Criteria: 28 days of service on naval vessels operating above the Arctic Circle
Devices: None

For participation in operations in support of the Arctic Warfare Program. The Navy Arctic Service Ribbon is worn after the Navy Sea Service Deployment Ribbon and before the Navy and Marine Corps Overseas Service Ribbon.

The Navy Arctic Service Ribbon was authorized by the Secretary of the Navy on 8 May 1986 and established by an OPNAVNOTE (Chief of Naval Operations Notice) on 3 June 1987. The ribbon is awarded to members of the Naval Service who participate in operations in support of the Arctic Warfare Program. To be eligible the individual must have served 28 days north of, or within 50 miles of the Marginal Ice Zone (MIZ). The MIZ is defined as an area consisting of more than 10% ice concentration.

The Navy Arctic Service Ribbon is a ribbon only award. The ribbon is medium blue with a narrow center stripe of navy blue flanked on either side by three thin stripes of gradually lighter shades of blue, a narrow stripe of white, followed again by two thin stripes of gradually darker shades of blue. There are no provisions for additional awards.

NAVY AND MARINE CORPS OVERSEAS SERVICE RIBBON

Silver　Bronze

Instituted: 1987
Criteria: 12 months consecutive or accumulated duty at an overseas shore base duty station
Devices: Bronze, silver star

For 12 months consecutive or accumulated active duty at an overseas duty station; or 30 consecutive days or 45 cumulative days of active duty for training or temporary active duty. The Navy and Marine Corps Overseas Service Ribbon is worn after the Navy Arctic Service Ribbon and before the Marine Corps Recruiting Ribbon.

The Navy and Marine Corps Overseas Service Ribbon was approved by the Secretary of the Navy and authorized by an OPNAVNOTE (Chief of Naval Operations Notice) on 3 June 1987 and made retroactive to 15 August 1974. The award is made to Active Duty Members of the Naval Service who serve 12 months at an overseas duty station. The ribbon is intended to recognize individuals who serve overseas, but are not members of ships, squadrons, or detachments of the Fleet Marine Force and do not qualify for the Navy Sea Service Deployment Ribbon. An individual cannot be awarded the Navy and Marine Corps Overseas Service Ribbon and the Navy Sea Service Deployment Ribbon for the same period of service.

The Navy and Marine Corps Overseas Service Ribbon is a ribbon only award. The ribbon has a wide red center stripe, bordered on either side by a thin yellow stripe, a wide navy blue stripe, a thin yellow stripe and a narrow medium blue border. Additional awards are denoted by three-sixteenth inch bronze stars.

MARINE CORPS RECRUITING RIBBON

☆　★
Silver　Bronze

Instituted: 1995
Criteria: Successful completion of 3 consecutive years of recruiting duty
Devices: Bronze, silver star

For the successful completion of three consecutive years of recruiting duty. The Marine Corps Recruiting Ribbon is worn after the Navy and Marine Corps Overseas Service Ribbon and before the Marine Corps Drill Instructor Ribbon.

The Marine Corps Recruiting Ribbon was established in 1995 and made retroactive to 1973. The ribbon is awarded to Marines who serve successfully in a three year recruiting assignment.

The Marine Corps Recruiting Ribbon is a ribbon only award. The ribbon is dark blue with a wide red center stripe. Additional awards are denoted by three-sixteenth inch bronze stars.

MARINE CORPS DRILL INSTRUCTOR RIBBON

Silver   Bronze

<u>Instituted:</u> 1997 - retroactive to 1952
<u>Criteria:</u> Successful completion of a tour of duty as a drill instructor (staff billets require completion of 18 months to be eligible).
<u>Devices:</u> Bronze, silver star

    For completion of a successful tour of duty as a drill instructor (MOS 8511). The Marine Corps Drill Instructor Ribbon is worn after the Marine Corps Recruiting Ribbon and before the Marine Security Guard Ribbon.

    The Marine Corps Drill Instructor Ribbon was established in 1997 and made retroactive to 6 October 1952. The ribbon is awarded to Marines who serve successfully in a drill instructor assignment. An assignment is defined as a tour of a minimum of 20 months for those who received their 8511 MOS before December 1996 or 30 months thereafter.

    The ribbon is also awarded to Marines who have successfully completed assignments of at least 18 cumulative months in the following billets:

Recruit Training Battalion -	Commanding Officer
	Executive Officer
	S-3 Officer
	Sergeant Major
Recruit Training Company - (Less Headquarters Company)	Commanding Officer
	Executive Officer
	First Sergeant
	Series Commander
Officer Candidate Company -	Commanding Officer
	Executive Officer
	First Sergeant
	Company Gunnery Sergeant
	Platoon Commanders

    The Marine Corps Drill Instructor Ribbon is a ribbon only award. The ribbon is dark olive green with a wide khaki tan center stripe. Additional awards are denoted by three-sixteenth inch bronze stars.

MARINE SECURITY GUARD RIBBON

Silver   Bronze

<u>Instituted:</u> 1997
<u>Criteria:</u> Successful completion of 24 months of cumulative security guard duty service at a foreign service establishment.
<u>Devices:</u> Bronze, silver star

    For the successful completion of two years of security guard duty. The Marine Security Guard Ribbon is worn after the Marine Corps Drill Instructor Ribbon and before the Armed Forces Reserve Medal.

    The Marine Security Guard Ribbon was established in 1997 and made retroactive to 28 January 1949, the date the first Marine Security Guards departed for overseas assignments. The ribbon is awarded to Marines assigned to Marine Security Guard duty (MOS 8151), who have successfully completed 24 months service at a foreign service establishment. Marines who served successful tours at a lettered company headquarters within MSGBn are also eligible to receive the ribbon upon completion of 24 months service.

    The Marine Security Guard Ribbon is a ribbon only award. The ribbon is medium blue with a narrow red center stripe bordered by bands of white. Additional awards are denoted by three-sixteenth inch bronze stars.

ARMED FORCES RESERVE MEDAL

Bronze, Bronze Bronze
Silver, Gold
Hourglass

Instituted: 1950
Criteria: 10 years of honorable service in any reserve
component of the United States Armed Forces
Devices: Bronze, silver and gold hourglass, bronze numeral and letter "M"

For ten years of honorable service in Reserve components of the Armed Forces. The Armed Forces Reserve Medal is worn after the Outstanding Volunteer Service Medal and before foreign medals when medals are worn and after the Marine Corps Security Guard Ribbon and before the Marine Corps Reserve Ribbon on a ribbon display.

The Armed Forces Reserve Medal was authorized by Executive Order on 25 September 1950 and amended on 19 March 1952. The medal is awarded to individuals who complete ten years of honorable satisfactory service in any of the reserve components, including the National Guard. The service does not need to be continuous, but the ten years must be completed within a twelve year period. Satisfactory service is defined as having been credited with a minimum of fifty reserve retirement points.

The Armed Forces Reserve Medal was designed by the Army's Institute of Heraldry. The medal is a circular bronze disc depicting a vertical flaming torch centered over a bugle and powder horn. In the background are thirteen stars and rays representing the thirteen original colonies. The reverse has the Marine Corps emblem around which is a raised circular inscription ARMED FORCES RESERVE. The ribbon is buff with a narrow medium blue center stripe and three thin medium blue stripes on each edge.

In certain cases, an early award of the Armed Forces Reserve Medal may be made. If a Reservist is called to active duty prior to the completion of the prescribed ten years of Reserve service, the medal is awarded immediately with a bronze letter "M" to denote the mobilization. Upon the completion of the ten year period, Reservists that are not mobilized are awarded the Armed Forces Reserve Medal with a bronze hourglass device. Silver and gold hourglass devices are awarded at the end of twenty and thirty years of Reserve service, respectively. Since only one letter "M" device may be awarded, a bronze numeral denotes the number of times the recipient has been mobilized for active duty.

MARINE CORPS RESERVE RIBBON

Bronze

Instituted: 1945
Dates: 1945-1965
Criteria: Successful completion of 10 years of honorable service in any class
of the Marine Corps Reserve
Devices: Bronze star

For ten years of service in the Marine Corps Reserve prior to 18 December 1965. The Marine Corps Reserve Ribbon is worn after the Armed Forces Reserve Medal and before any foreign awards.

The Marine Corps Reserve Ribbon was authorized by the Secretary of the Navy on 17 December 1945. The medal was awarded to members of the Marine Corps Reserve for ten years of honorable service prior to 18 December 1965, at which time it was superseded by the Armed Forces Reserve Medal. Service counted in completing the required time for the Selected Marine Corps Reserve Medal or the Armed Forces Reserve Medal is not eligible for this award. A Marine Reservist who is eligible for these three awards may elect which one of these awards he or she will receive.

The Marine Corps Reserve Ribbon is a ribbon only award. The ribbon is gold with a thin stripe of red at each edge. A three-sixteenth inch bronze star is authorized for a second, ten-year period of Marine Corps Reserve service.

FOREIGN DECORATIONS

Foreign decorations are worn positioned after U.S. awards. If an individual is authorized awards from more than one country, the awards should be worn in the order earned; for more than one award from the same country, the awards should be worn in the order of precedence established by that country.

THE REPUBLIC OF VIETNAM STAFF SERVICE MEDAL

Instituted: 1964
Criteria: Staff services evidencing outstanding initiative
Devices: None

Awarded by the Republic of Vietnam to members of the U.S. Armed Forces for outstanding staff work.

The Republic of Vietnam Staff Service Medal is a foreign award. The medal was authorized on 12 May 1964. This medal was awarded by the Republic of Vietnam to members of the U.S. Armed Forces for staff service who evidenced outstanding initiative and devotion to duty. This medal was widely awarded to American advisors.

The Republic of Vietnam Staff Service Medal is a gold square fortress design with bastions at each point, suspended from one point, with a sword and a writing brush crossed underneath. In the center is a blue diamond with gold crossed rifles, wings and an anchor. The back of the medal has a stamped circle THAM-MUU BOI-TINH VIET-NAM with a small four pointed star in the center. The medal comes in two classes: First Class for officers with a green ribbon with red and white diagonal stripes and Second Class for enlisted personnel with a blue ribbon with red and white stripes.

For more information on Vietnamese decorations and medals see *The Decorations and Medals of the Republic of Vietnam and Her Allies 1950-1975*.

PHILIPPINE REPUBLIC PRESIDENTIAL UNIT CITATION

Bronze

Instituted: 1948
Criteria: Awarded to units of the U.S. Armed Forces for service in the war against Japan and/or for 1970 and 1972 disaster relief
Devices: Bronze star

For service in a unit cited in the name of the President of the Republic of the Philippines for outstanding performance in action.

The Philippine Republic Presidential Unit Citation is a foreign award. It was awarded to members of the Armed Forces of the United States for services resulting in the liberation of the Philippines during World War II. The award was made in the name of the President of the Republic of the Philippines and the criteria is the same as for the Presidential Unit Citation of the United States. The Philippine Presidential Unit Citation was also awarded to U.S. Forces who participated in disaster relief operations 1 August 1970 to 14 December 1970 and 21 July 1972 to 15 August 1972.

The Philippine Republic Presidential Unit Citation is a ribbon only award. The ribbon has three wide stripes of blue, white and red enclosed in a rectangular one-sixteenth inch gold frame with laurel leaves. A three-sixteenth inch bronze star is authorized for a recipient who received more than one award.

REPUBLIC OF KOREA PRESIDENTIAL UNIT CITATION

Instituted: 1951
Criteria: Awarded to certain units of the U.S. Armed Forces for services rendered during the Korean War
Devices: None
Notes: Above date devotes when award was authorized for wear by U.S. Armed Forces personnel

Awarded by the Republic of Korea for service in a unit cited in the name of the President of the Republic of Korea for outstanding performance in action.

The Republic of Korea Presidential Unit Citation is a foreign award. It was awarded to units of the United Nations Command for service in Korea during the Korean Conflict from 1950 to 1954. The award was made in the name of the President of the Republic of Korea and the criteria is the same as for the Presidential Unit Citation of the United States.

The Republic Korea Presidential Unit Citation is a ribbon only award. The ribbon is white bordered with a wide green stripe and thin stripes of white, red, white, red, white and green. In the center is an ancient oriental symbol called a tae-guk (the top half is red and the bottom half is blue). The ribbon is enclosed in a rectangular one-sixteenth inch gold frame with laurel leaves.

REPUBLIC OF VIETNAM PRESIDENTIAL UNIT CITATION (FRIENDSHIP RIBBON)

Instituted: 1954
Criteria: Awarded to certain units of the U.S. Armed Forces for humanitarian service in the evacuation of civilians from North and Central Vietnam
Devices: None
Notes: Above date devotes when award was authorized for wear by U.S. Armed Forces personnel

Awarded by the Republic of Vietnam for service in a unit cited in the name of the President of the Republic of Vietnam for outstanding performance in action.

The Republic of Vietnam Presidential Unit Citation is a foreign award. Referred to as the "Friendship Ribbon", it was awarded to members of the United States Military Assistance Advisory Group in Indo-China for services rendered during August and September 1954. The ribbon is awarded in the name of the President of the Republic of Vietnam.

The Republic of Vietnam Presidential Unit Citation is a ribbon only award. The ribbon is yellow with three narrow red stripes in the center. The ribbon is enclosed in a rectangular one-sixteenth inch gold frame with laurel leaves.

REPUBLIC OF VIETNAM GALLANTRY CROSS UNIT CITATION

Bronze Palm

Instituted: 1966
Criteria: Awarded to certain units of the U.S. Armed Forces for valorous combat achievement during the Vietnam War, 1 March 1961 to 28 March 1974
Devices: Bronze palm
Notes: Above date devotes when award was authorized for wear by U.S. Armed Forces personnel

Awarded by the Republic of Vietnam to units of the U.S. Armed Forces in recognition of valorous achievement in combat during the Vietnam War (1 March 1961-28 March 1974).

The Republic of Vietnam Gallantry Cross Unit Citation was established on 15 August 1950. The ribbon was awarded to units by the Republic of Vietnam for the same services as would be required for the Navy Unit Commendation.

The Republic of Vietnam Gallantry Cross Unit Citation is a foreign award. The ribbon is red with a very wide yellow center stripe, which has eight very thin double red stripes. The ribbon bar is enclosed in a one-sixteenth inch gold frame with laurel leaves. A bronze palm device is attached to the ribbon.

For more information on Vietnamese decorations and medals see *The Decorations and Medals of the Republic of Vietnam and Her Allies 1950-1975*.

REPUBLIC OF VIETNAM CIVIL ACTIONS UNIT CITATION

Bronze Palm

Instituted: 1966
Criteria: Awarded to certain units of the U.S. Armed Forces for meritorious service during the Vietnam War, 1 March 1961 to 28 March 1974
Devices: Bronze palm

Awarded by the Republic of Vietnam to units in recognition of meritorious civil action service.

The Republic of Vietnam Civil Actions Unit Citation, sometimes called the Civic Actions Honor Medal, was widely bestowed on American forces in Vietnam as a unit citation for which there is no medal authorized. The award recognizes outstanding achievements made by units in the field of civil affairs.

The Republic of Vietnam Civil Actions Unit Citation is a foreign award. The ribbon is dark green with a very thin double red center stripe narrow red stripes near the edges. The ribbon is enclosed in a rectangular one-sixteenth inch gold frame with laurel leaves and is normally awarded with a bronze laurel leaf palm attachment.

For more information on Vietnamese decorations and medals see *The Decorations and Medals of the Republic of Vietnam and Her Allies 1950-1975*.

PHILIPPINE DEFENSE MEDAL AND RIBBON

Bronze

Country: Republic of the Philippines
Instituted: 1945
Criteria: Service in defense of the Philippines between 8 December 1941 and 15 June 1942
Devices: Bronze star

Awarded by the Philippine Commonwealth for service in defense of the Philippines.

The Philippine Defense Ribbon was authorized in 1945 by the United States and the Philippine Commonwealth governments. The ribbon was awarded to members of the United States Armed Forces for service in the defense of the Philippines from 8 December 1941 to 15 June 1942.

The Philippine Defense Ribbon is a foreign award. Although not authorized for wear on the U.S. military uniform, a medal was designed and struck by the Philippine Government. The medal was designed by the Manila firm of El Oro. The medal is a circular gold disc with an outer edge of ten scallops. At the medal's center is a female figure with a sword and shield representing the Philippines. Above the figure are three stars and surrounding it is a green enamel wreath. At the bottom right of the medal is a map of Corregidor and Bataan. At the bottom left is a floral design. The reverse of the medal has the raised inscription FOR THE DEFENSE OF THE PHILIPPINES set in four lines. The ribbon is red with two white stripes near the edges and three white five-pointed stars in the center. A three-sixteenth inch bronze star denotes additional service during the prescribed eligibility period.

PHILIPPINE LIBERATION MEDAL AND RIBBON

Bronze

<u>Country:</u> Republic of the Philippines
<u>Instituted:</u> 1945
<u>Criteria:</u> Service in the liberation of the Philippines between 17 October 1944 and 3 September 1945
<u>Devices:</u> Bronze star

Awarded by the Philippine Commonwealth for the liberation of the Philippines.

The Philippine Liberation Ribbon was authorized for members of the Naval Service by ALNAV 64 on 5 April 1945. The ribbon was awarded to members of the United States Armed Forces for service in the liberation of the Philippines from 17 October 1944 to 3 September 1945.

The Philippine Defense Ribbon is a foreign award. Although not authorized for wear on the U.S. military uniform, a medal was designed and struck by the Philippine Government The medal was designed by the Manila firm of El Oro. The medal is gold with a Philippine sword, point up, superimposed over a white native shield. The shield has three gold stars at the top and the word LIBERTY below. Below are vertical stripes of blue, white and red enamel with the sword being in the center of the white stripe. At the sides of the medal and below the shield are gold arched wings. The reverse of the medal has the raised inscription FOR THE LIBERATION OF THE PHILIPPINES set in four lines. The ribbon is red with narrow blue stripe and a narrow white stripe in the center. Three-sixteenth inch bronze stars (up to two) denote additional service during the prescribed eligibility period.

PHILIPPINE INDEPENDENCE MEDAL AND RIBBON

<u>Country:</u> Republic of the Philippines
<u>Instituted:</u> 1946
<u>Criteria:</u> Receipt of both the Philippine Defense and Liberation Medals/Ribbons. Originally presented to those present for duty in the Philippines on 4 July 1946
<u>Devices:</u> None

Awarded by the Philippine Commonwealth to those members of the Armed Forces who received both the Philippine Defense Ribbon and the Philippine Liberation Ribbon.

The Philippine Independence Ribbon was authorized in 1946 by the United States and the Philippine Commonwealth. The ribbon was presented to those members of the United States Armed Forces who were serving in the Philippines on 4 July 1946 or who were previously awarded the Philippine Defense Ribbon and the Philippine Liberation Ribbon.

The Philippine Independence Ribbon is a foreign award. Although not authorized to be worn on the U.S. military uniform, a medal was designed and struck by the Philippine Government. The medal was designed by the Manila firm of El Oro. The medal is a circular gold disc with a female figure in the center, dressed in native garb and holding the Philippine flag. There are flags on either side of the figure and she is surrounded by a circular border. Inside the border is a raised inscription PHILIPPINE INDEPENDENCE around the top and July 4 1946 at the bottom. The ribbon is medium blue with a narrow white center stripe bordered by thin red stripes. There are thin yellow stripes at each edge.

UNITED NATIONS SERVICE MEDAL (KOREA)

Instituted: 1951
Criteria: Service on behalf of the United Nations in Korea between 27 June 1950 and 27 July 1954
Devices: None
Notes: Above date denotes when award was authorized for wear by U.S. Armed Forces personnel

For service on behalf of the United Nations in Korea during the Korean Conflict.

The United Nations Service Medal is a foreign award. It was authorized by the United Nations General Assembly on 12 December 1950 and the Department of Defense approved it for United States Armed Forces on 27 November 1951. The medal was awarded to any member of the United States Armed Forces for service in support of the United Nations Command during the period from 27 June 1950 to 27 July 1954. Individuals who were awarded the Korean Service Medal automatically established eligibility for this decoration.

The United Nations Service Medal was designed by the United Nations. The medal is a circular bronze disc with the United Nations emblem (a polar projection of the world taken from the North Pole, encircled by two olive branches). The reverse of the medal has the raised inscription FOR SERVICE IN DEFENSE OF THE PRINCIPLES OF THE CHARTER OF THE UNITED NATIONS set in five lines. The medal is suspended permanently from a bar, similar to British medals, with the raised inscription KOREA. The ribbon passes through the bar and is narrow stripes of alternating light blue and white.

UNITED NATIONS MEDAL

Bronze

Instituted: 1964
Criteria: 6 months service with any U.N. peacekeeping mission
Devices: Bronze star
Notes: Above date denotes when award was authorized for wear by U.S. Armed Forces personnel

For six months service on behalf of the United Nations in one of eleven missions (see page 94 and 95).

The United Nations Medal is a non-U.S. service award. It was authorized by the United Nations General Assembly on 30 July 1959 and approved by Executive Order on 11 March 1964. The medal was awarded to any member of the United States Armed Forces for not less than six months service in support of a United Nations missions (UNTSO).

The United Nations Medal was designed by the United Nations. The medal is a bronze disc with the United Nations emblem (a polar projection of the world taken from the North Pole, encircled by two olive branches). Centered above this are the letters UN. The reverse of the medal has the raised inscription IN THE SERVICE OF PEACE. The medallion for all UN operations is the same for all authorized operations. The basic ribbon is United Nations blue with narrow stripes of white near the edges, however each authorized operation has a unique ribbon. Individuals who have participated in more than one UN operation wear only the first medal for which they qualify with a three-sixteenth inch bronze star for each subsequent award.

United Nations Missions Participated in by United States Armed Forces Personnel

Until recently Marine personnel serving on or with a United Nations mission were permitted to wear two UN medals. The UN medal from Korean service and UNTSO (UN Truce Supervision Organization) medal.

A change in Department of Defense regulations now authorizes military personnel to wear the ribbon of one of 11 UN missions. Only one UN ribbon may be worn. Subsequent mission awards are denoted by three-sixteenth inch bronze stars on the earned UN ribbon.

The United States has participated in 15 UN Missions (as of the date this book was published). To date there are 11 medals authorized for U.S. military personnel. The eleven medals currently authorized are shown below. *(The United Nations Special Service Medal is also shown)*

1. **UNTSO - UNITED NATIONS TRUCE SUPERVISION ORGANIZATION**
   <u>COUNTRY/LOCATION:</u> Palestine/Israel
   <u>DATES:</u> June 1948 to present
   <u>COUNTRIES PARTICIPATING:</u> (20) Argentina, Australia, Austria, Belgium, Canada, Chile, China, Denmark, Finland, France, Ireland, Italy, Myanmar, Netherlands, New Zealand, Norway, Sweden, Switzerland, United States, USSR
   <u>MAXIMUM STRENGTH:</u> 572 military observers (1948)
   <u>CURRENT STRENGTH:</u> 178 (1996)
   <u>FATALITIES:</u> 38 (1996)   <u>CLASP(S):</u> **CONGO, UNGOMAP, OSGAP**

2. **UNMOGIP - UNITED NATIONS MILITARY OBSERVER GROUP IN INDIA AND PAKISTAN**
   <u>COUNTRY/LOCATION:</u> India, Pakistan (Jammu & Kashmir)
   <u>DATES:</u> January 1949 to present
   <u>COUNTRIES PARTICIPATING:</u> (15) Australia, Belgium, Canada, Chile, Denmark, Ecuador, Finland, Italy, Korean Republic, Mexico, New Zealand, Norway, Sweden, United States, Uruguay
   <u>MAXIMUM STRENGTH:</u> 102 military observers (1965)
   <u>CURRENT STRENGTH:</u> 44 (1996)   <u>FATALITIES:</u> 9 (1996)   <u>CLASP(S):</u> None

3. **KOREA - UNITED NATIONS KOREAN SERVICE**
   <u>COUNTRY/LOCATION:</u> Korea   <u>DATES:</u> June 1950 to July 1953
   <u>COUNTRIES PARTICIPATING:</u> (19) Australia, Belgium, Canada, Colombia, Ethiopia, France, Greece, Luxembourg, Netherlands, New Zealand, Philippines, South Korea, Thailand, Turkey, Union of South Africa, United Kingdom, United States (plus Denmark and Italy which provided medical support)
   <u>MAXIMUM STRENGTH (approx):</u> 1,000,000 (UN & South Korea combined)
   <u>CURRENT STRENGTH:</u> ---------
   <u>FATALITIES (approx):</u> Korea: 415,000, U.S.: 55,000, Other UN: 3,100   <u>CLASP(S):</u> None

4. **UNSF - UNITED NATIONS SECURITY FORCE IN WEST NEW GUINEA (WEST IRIAN)**
   UNTEA - UNITED NATIONS TEMPORARY EXECUTIVE AUTHORITY
   <u>COUNTRY/LOCATION:</u> West Irian (West New Guinea)
   <u>DATES:</u> October 1962 to April 1963
   <u>COUNTRIES PARTICIPATING:</u> (9) Brazil, Canada, Ceylon, India, Ireland, Nigeria, Pakistan, Sweden, United States
   <u>MAXIMUM STRENGTH:</u> 1,576 military observers (1963)
   <u>STRENGTH AT WITHDRAWAL:</u> 1,576
   <u>FATALITIES:</u> None
   <u>CLASP(S):</u> None

5. **UNIKOM - UNITED NATIONS IRAQ-KUWAIT OBSERVATION MISSION**
   <u>COUNTRY/LOCATION:</u> Iraq, Kuwait   <u>DATES:</u> April 1991 to present
   <u>COUNTRIES PARTICIPATING:</u> (36) Argentina, Austria, Bangladesh, Canada, Chile, China, Denmark, Fiji, Finland, France, Germany, Ghana, Greece, Hungary, India, Indonesia, Ireland, Italy, Kenya, Malaysia, Nigeria, Norway, Pakistan, Poland, Romania, Russian Federation, Senegal, Singapore, Sweden, Switzerland, Thailand, Turkey, United Kingdom, United States, Uruguay, Venezuela
   <u>MAXIMUM STRENGTH:</u> 1,187 military observers   <u>CURRENT STRENGTH:</u> 1,179 (1996)
   <u>FATALITIES:</u> 6 (1996)
   <u>CLASP(S):</u> None

6. MINURSO - UNITED NATIONS MISSION FOR THE REFERENDUM IN WESTERN SAHARA
COUNTRY/LOCATION: Western Sahara (Morocco) DATES: September 1991 to present
COUNTRIES PARTICIPATING: (36) Argentina, Australia, Austria, Bangladesh, Belgium, Canada, China, Egypt, El Salvador, Finland, France, Germany, Ghana, Greece, Guinea-Bissau, Honduras, Hungary, Ireland, Italy, Kenya, Korean Republic, Malaysia, Nigeria, Norway, Pakistan, Peru, Poland, Portugal, Russian Federation, Switzerland, Togo, Tunisia, United Kingdom, United States, Uruguay, Venezuela
MAXIMUM STRENGTH: 3,000 authorized (1,700 military observers and troops, 300 police officers, approx. 1,000 civilian personnel)
CURRENT STRENGTH: 352 (1996)   FATALITIES: 7 (1996)   CLASP(S): None

7. UNAMIC - UNITED NATIONS ADVANCE MISSION IN CAMBODIA
COUNTRY/LOCATION: Cambodia
DATES: November 1991 to March 1992
COUNTRIES PARTICIPATING: (24) Algeria, Argentina, Australia, Austria, Belgium, Canada, China, France, Germany, Ghana, India, Indonesia, Ireland, Malaysia, New Zealand, Pakistan, Poland, Russian Federation, Senegal, Thailand, Tunisia, United Kingdom, United States, Uruguay
MAXIMUM STRENGTH: 1,090 military and civilian personnel (1992)
STRENGTH AT TRANSITION TO UNTAC: 1,090   FATALITIES: None

8. UNPROFOR - UNITED NATIONS PROTECTION FORCE
COUNTRY/LOCATION: Former Yugoslavia (Bosnia, Herzegovina, Croatia, Serbia, Montenegro, Macedonia)
DATES: March 1992 to December 1995
COUNTRIES PARTICIPATING: (43) Argentina, Australia, Bangladesh, Belgium, Brazil, Canada, Colombia, Czech Republic, Denmark, Egypt, Finland, France, Germany, Ghana, India, Indonesia, Ireland, Jordan, Kenya, Lithuania, Luxembourg, Malaysia, Nepal, Netherlands, New Zealand, Nigeria, Norway, Pakistan, Poland, Portugal, Russian Federation, Senegal, Slovakia, Spain, Sweden, Switzerland, Thailand, Tunisia, Turkey, Ukraine, United Kingdom, United States, Venezuela
MAXIMUM STRENGTH: 39,922 (38,614 troops and support personnel, 637 military observers, 671 civilian police and 4,058 staff (1994)
STRENGTH AT WITHDRAWAL: 2,675   FATALITIES: 207   CLASP(S): None

9. UNTAC - UNITED NATIONS TRANSITIONAL AUTHORITY IN CAMBODIA
LOCATION: Cambodia   DATES: Mar. 1992 to Sept. 1993
COUNTRIES PARTICIPATING: (46) Algeria, Argentina, Australia, Austria, Bangladesh, Belgium, Brunei, Bulgaria, Cameroon, Canada, Chile, China, Colombia, Egypt, Fiji, France, Germany, Ghana, Hungary, India, Indonesia, Ireland, Italy, Japan, Jordan, Kenya, Malaysia, Morocco, Namibia, Nepal, Netherlands, New Zealand, Nigeria, Norway, Pakistan, Philippines, Poland, Russian Federation, Senegal, Singapore, Sweden, Thailand, Tunisia, United Kingdom, United States, Uruguay
MAXIMUM STRENGTH: 19,350 military and civilian personnel (1993)
STRENGTH AT WITHDRAWAL: 2,500 (approx.)   FATALITIES: 78   CLASP(S): UNAMIC (later withdrawn)

10. UNOSOM II - UNITED NATIONS OPERATION IN SOMALIA II
COUNTRY/LOCATION: Somalia   DATES: May 1993 to March 1995
COUNTRIES PARTICIPATING: (34) Australia, Bangladesh, Belgium, Botswana, Canada, Egypt, France, Germany, Ghana, Greece, India, Indonesia, Ireland, Italy, Korean Republic, Kuwait, Malaysia, Morocco, Nepal, Netherlands, New Zealand, Nigeria, Norway, Pakistan, Philippines, Romania, Saudi Arabia, Sweden, Tunisia, Turkey, United Arab Emirates, United States, Zambia, Zimbabwe
MAXIMUM STRENGTH: 30,800 authorized (28,000 military personnel and approximately 2,800 civilian staff)
STRENGTH AT WITHDRAWAL: 14,968   FATALITIES: 147   CLASP(S): None

11. UNMIH - UNITED NATIONS MISSION IN HAITI
COUNTRY/LOCATION: Haiti   DATES: Sept 1993 to June 1996
COUNTRIES PARTICIPATING: (34) Algeria, Antigua and Barbuda, Argentina, Austria, Bahamas, Bangladesh, Barbados, Belize, Benin, Canada, Djibouti, France, Guatemala, Guinea-Bissau, Guyana, Honduras, India, Ireland, Jamaica, Jordan, Mali. Nepal, Netherlands, New Zealand, Pakistan, Philippines, Russian Federation, St.Kitts & Nevis, St.Lucia, Suriname, Togo, Trinidad and Tobago, Tunisia, United States
MAXIMUM STRENGTH: 6,065 military personnel and 847 civilian police (1995)
STRENGTH AT TRANSITION TO UNSMIH: 1,200 troops and 300 civilian police
FATALITIES: 6   CLASP(S): None

UNSSM - UNITED NATIONS SPECIAL SERVICE MEDAL
BACKGROUND: Established in 1994 by the Secretary-General of the United Nations, the United Nations Medal for Special Service is awarded to military and civilian police personnel serving the United Nations in capacities other than established peace-keeping missions or those permanently assigned to United Nations Headquarters (see medal 44 above). The Medal for Special Service may be awarded to eligible personnel serving for a minimum of ninety (90) consecutive days under the control of the United Nations in operations or offices for which no other United Nations award is authorized. Posthumous awards may be granted to personnel otherwise eligible for the medal who die while serving under the United Nations before completing the required 90 consecutive days of service.
CLASP(S): Clasps engraved with the name of the country or the United Nations organization (e.g., UNHCR, UNSCOM, MINUGUA, etc.) may be added to the medal suspension ribbon and ribbon bar.

NATO MEDAL

Bronze

<u>Instituted:</u> 1992
<u>Criteria:</u> 30 days service in or 90 days outside the former Republic of Yugoslavia and the Adriatic Sea under NATO command in direct support of NATO operations
<u>Devices:</u> None
<u>Notes:</u> Above date denotes when award was authorized for wear by U.S. military personnel.
"Former Yugoslavia" Bar not authorized for wear by U.S. Armed Forces personnel.

Awarded by The North Atlantic Treaty Organization (NATO) to military personnel who have served under NATO command or in direct support of NATO operations.

The NATO Medal is a non-U.S. service award. The medal is awarded to members of the U.S. Armed Forces who served 30 days under NATO command, or 90 days in direct support of NATO operations in the former Republic of Yugoslavia and the Adriatic Sea, or as designated by SACEUR from 1 July 1992 to a date currently undetermined.

The NATO Medal is a circular bronze disc with a raised edge. In the center of the medal is the NATO star surrounded by a wreath of olive leaves. The reverse of the medal contains the raised inscription IN SERVICE OF PEACE AND FREEDOM in both English (on top) and in French (below). Around the edge is a raised double ring with the enclosed inscription NORTH ATLANTIC TREATY ORGANIZATION in both English (on top) and in French (below). The ribbon is medium blue with narrow light blue stripe near the edges. The medal is sometimes issued with a clasp, which it is not worn by U.S. Armed Forces. Additional awards will be denoted by three sixteenth-inch bronze stars.

MULTINATIONAL FORCE and OBSERVERS MEDAL

Bronze Numeral

<u>Instituted:</u> 1982
<u>Criteria:</u> 90/170 days service with the Multinational Force & Observers peacekeeping force in the Sinai Desert
<u>Devices:</u> Bronze numeral
<u>Notes:</u> Above date denotes when award was authorized for wear by U.S. Armed Forces personnel

For service with the Multinational Force and Observers peacekeeping force in the Sinai Desert. The Multinational Force and Observers was created to act as a buffer between Israel and Egypt in the Sinai Peninsula.

The Multinational Force and Observers Medal is a non-U.S. service award. The award was established on 24 March 1982. Approval for US personnel to wear this decoration was granted by the Department of Defense on 26 July 1982. The medal was first awarded to individuals who served at least 90 days with the Multinational Force and Observers. The time of service was increased to 170 days minimum after 15 March 1985. The medal was instituted to recognize those who participated in the Mideast peacekeeping process.

The Multinational Force and Observers Medal is a bronze circular disc depicting a dove and an olive branch centered within two raised rings. Between the two rings is the raised inscription MULTINATIONAL FORCE at the top, and & OBSERVERS at the bottom. There is a fine grid pattern in the background. The medal is suspended from a bronze rectangular bar, which is attached to the ribbon. The reverse of the medal has the raised inscription UNITED IN SERVICE FOR PEACE set in five straight lines. The ribbon is orange with a wide white center stripe flanked on each side with narrow olive green stripes. Bronze numerals are authorized for subsequent awards.

INTER-AMERICAN DEFENSE BOARD MEDAL

Gold

Instituted: 1981
Criteria: Service with the Inter-American Defense Board for at least one year
Devices: Gold star
Notes: Above date denotes when award was authorized for wear by U.S. military personnel

For service of a minimum of one year on the Inter-American Defense Board.

The Inter-American Defense Board Medal is a non-U.S. service award. The medal was authorized by the Inter-American Defense Board on 11 December 1945 and authorized for the Armed Forces of the United States by the Department of Defense on 12 May 1981. The criteria for the award is a minimum of one year service on the board in specific responsibilities.

The Inter-American Defense Board Medal is a circular bronze disc with a map projection of the Western Hemisphere in the center. Around the projection are the flags of the Nations of North and South America. The reverse of the medal is blank, but when presented it is engraved with the recipients name and the words FROM THE INTER-AMERICAN DEFENSE BOARD and FOR SERVICE. The ribbon is five equal stripes of red, white, blue, yellow and green. An additional period of service on the Inter-American Defense Board is denoted by a five-sixteenth inch gold star.

REPUBLIC OF VIETNAM CAMPAIGN MEDAL

Silver Date Bar

Instituted: 1966
Criteria: 6 months service in the Republic of Vietnam between 1961 and 1973 or if wounded, captured or killed in action during the above period
Devices: Silver date bar
Notes: Bar inscribed "1960- " is the only authorized version

Awarded by the Republic of Vietnam to members of the U.S. Armed Forces who served for six months in Vietnam.

The Republic of Vietnam Campaign Medal is a foreign award. The medal was authorized on 20 July 1966 and amended on 31 January 1974. This campaign medal was awarded by the Republic of Vietnam to members of the U.S Armed Forces who served a minimum of six months in the Republic of Vietnam between 1 March 1961 and 28 March 1973, or who had provided direct combat support to the RVN during the period of the award. The Government of Vietnam awarded the ribbon, but the medal must be purchased by recipients. Anyone qualifying for the Vietnam Service Medal was automatically awarded this medal.

The Republic of Vietnam Campaign Medal is a six pointed white enamel star, bordered in gold, with cut lined broad gold star points between. In the center of the star is a green disc, bordered in gold, with a map of Vietnam in gold and a red enamel flame. The reverse of the medal has a raised inscription VIETNAM in a lined circle with CHIEN-DICH at the top and BOI-TINH below separated by short lines. The ribbon is green with a white center stripe an white stripes near the edges. A silver scroll is attached to the ribbon with the date 1960 and a dash.

KUWAIT LIBERATION MEDAL (SAUDI ARABIA)

Gold Palm Tree

Instituted: 1991
Criteria: Participation in, or support of, Operation Desert Storm (1990-91)
Devices: Gold palm tree device
Notes: Support must have been performed in theater (e.g.: Persian Gulf, Red Sea, Iraq, Kuwait, Saudi Arabia, Gulf of Oman, etc.)

Awarded by the Kingdom of Saudi Arabia for participation in Operation Desert Storm.

The Kuwait Liberation Medal (Saudi Arabia) is a foreign award. The medal was authorized for wear by members of the U.S. Armed Forces by the Department of Defense on 7 October 1991. This medal was awarded by the Kingdom of Saudi Arabia to their troops and troops of the United Nations Coalition who served in the Kuwait war zone from 17 January to 28 February 1991.

The Kuwait Liberation Medal (Saudi Arabia) was designed by the Swiss firm of Huguenin Medailleurs. The medal consists of a silver star with fifteen large rays and fifteen small rays. In the center of the star is a disc with a gold map of Kuwait on a silver globe surrounded by two palm branches. Above the globe is a royal crown and above that are crossed swords and a palm tree, which is the emblem of Saudi Arabia. At the bottom of the design is a scroll with the raised inscription LIBERATION OF KUWAIT in Arabic and in English. The ribbon has a dark green center stripe flanked on either side by a narrow white stripe and a thin black stripe. The ribbon is edged with a narrow red stripe. The ribbon bar employs the emblem of Saudi Arabia (crossed swords and a palm tree) in the center.

KUWAIT LIBERATION MEDAL (EMIRATE OF KUWAIT)

Instituted: 1995
Criteria: Participation in, or support of, Operations Desert Shield and/or Desert Storm
Devices: None
Notes: Above date denotes when award was authorized for wear by U.S. Armed Forces personnel

Awarded by the Kuwaiti Government for participation in Operation Desert Shield and Desert Storm.

The Kuwait Liberation Medal (Emirate of Kuwait) was authorized for wear by members of the U.S. Armed Forces by the Department of Defense in March 1995. This medal was awarded by the Kuwaiti Government for service in Operation Desert Shield and Desert Storm during the period from 2 August 1990 to 31 August 1993. Personnel must have served a minimum of one day on the ground, one day at sea, one day in aerial operations, or temporary duty of 30 days consecutive/60 days non-consecutive in support of military operations in the area.

The Kuwait Liberation Medal (Emirate of Kuwait) is a circular bronze disc with the Coat of Arms of the State of Kuwait. The Coat of Arms consists of the Shield of Kuwait in black, red, white and green enamel superimposed on a falcon with wings spread. Between the falcon's up-spread wings is a disk containing a sailing ship with the name of state above it. At the top of the medal is a raised Arabic inscription 1991 LIBERATION MEDAL. The medal is suspended by a wreath attached to a bronze rectangle which is attached to the suspension ribbon. The reverse of the medal has a map of Kuwait over a background of rays. The ribbon has three wide vertical stripes of red, white and green below a wide horizontal trapezoidal-shaped black stripe.

"GEORGE" MEDAL

The "George" Medal is legendary among 1st Marine Division veterans of Guadalcanal. It commemorates the difficult situation the Division experienced during the early days on Guadalcanal, when ammunition and food were short and Japanese were plentiful.

The medal was designed by then - Captain Donald L. Dickson, Adjutant of the 5th Marines at the direction of General (then Colonel) Merrill B. Twining, G-3 of the 1st Marine Division. Twining resolved to commemorate the D-Day plus three Navy withdrawal in the face of increasing Japanese air attacks and surface action, which left the Division in such tough shape. Twining told Dickson in general terms what he had in mind and Dickson designed the medal using a fifty-cent piece to draw a circle on a captured Japanese blank military postcard.

After Dickson's design was approved and the Division got to Australia, a mold was made by a local craftsman and a small number of medals were struck before the mold became unserviceable. These particular medals are very rare since only about 50 (some say as few as 20) were cast. The medal is a circular bronze disc that depicts a hand in a sleeve dropping a hot potato in the shape of Guadalcanal into the arms of a "grateful" Marine. In the original design the sleeve supposedly bore the stripes of a Vice Admiral intended to be either Vice Admiral Robert L. Ghormley, ComSoPac, or Vice Admiral Frank Jack Fletcher, Commander, Joint Expeditionary Force, who left the Marines without their heavy artillery and logistical support. The final design diplomatically omitted this identification. The obverse also shows a barrel cactus, hardly indigenous to Guadalcanal, but the code name for the operation was "Cactus". The Latin inscription is FACIAT GEORGIUS, "Let George Do It", thus, the George Medal. The medal's reverse pictures a cow (the original design showed a Japanese soldier) and an electric fan and is inscribed IN FOND REMEMBRANCE OF HAPPY DAYS SPENT FROM AUG. 7TH 1942 TO JAN. 5TH 1943, U.S.M.C. The ribbon was made, appropriately, of the pale green herringbone twill from some Marine's utility uniform. Legend has it that to be authentic, the utilities from which the ribbons were made had to have been washed in the waters of Guadalcanal's Lunga River. Some of the medals were provided with an oversized safety pin used to identify laundry bags in Navy shipboard laundries. This is not an authorized medal for wear on the uniform.

The George Medal shown in this book was donated to the Marine Corps Museum by Brigadier General James J. Keating, USMC (Ret.), who commanded the 3rd Battalion, 11th Marines, the last 1st Marine Division unit to leave Guadalcanal, 5 January 1943.

(Obverse)

(Reverse)

Displaying Awards

In the United States, it is quite rare for an individual to wear full-size medals once he or she is no longer on active duty. Unfortunately, many veterans return to civilian life with little concern for the state of their awards. In the euphoria of the moment, medals are tucked away in corners or children play with them, often causing irreparable damage to these noble mementos of a man's or woman's patriotic deeds. The loss or damage of these medals is sad, since awards reflect the veteran's part in American History and are totally unique and personal to each family.

The most appropriate use of military medals after active service is to mount the medals for permanent display in home or office. This reflects the individual's patriotism and the service rendered the United States. Unfortunately, there are very few first class companies in the United States which possess the expertise to properly prepare and mount awards and other personal militaria. The following pages provide examples of the formats, mounting methods and configurations employed by Medals of America in Fountain Inn, South Carolina to display military decorations. The examples range from World War II, Korea, Vietnam and Kuwait to peacetime service.

Decorations are usually awarded in a presentation set which normally consists of a medal, ribbon bar and lapel pin, all contained in a special case. During World War II, the name of the decoration was stamped in gold on the front of the case. However, as budget considerations assumed greater importance, this practice was gradually phased out and replaced by a standard case with "United States of America" emblazoned on the front.

At the present time, the more common decorations, (e.g.: Achievement and Commendation Medals), come in small plastic cases, suitable only for initial presentation and storage of the medal. Using this case in its open position for prolonged display exposes the entire presentation set to dust, acids and other atmospheric contaminants which can cause tarnish and/or serious discoloration.

Outside the case, medals and ribbons should be handled as little as possible, since oils and dirt on the hands can cause oxidation on the pendant and staining of the ribbon.

The most effective method of protecting awards involves the use of a shadow box or glass display case with at least 1/2 inch between the medals and the glass. This provides a three dimensional view and protects the medal display in a dust-free environment. Cases which press the medals and ribbons against the glass can disfigure the ribbon, cause discoloration and, in some extreme cases, damage the medal.

The greatest mistake an ordinary frame shop can make is in the actual process of mounting the medals. They often clip off prongs or pins on the back of a medal to ease the task of gluing the medal to a flat surface. The physical alteration destroys the integrity of the medal and the use of glues ruins the back of the ribbon and medal. The net result, ignoring the intrinsic value of the piece, is serious damage to a valued heirloom and keepsake.

The best way to mount medals is in a wooden case especially designed for that purpose. They can be obtained either with a fold-out easel back for placement on a table, desk or mantle, or with a notched hook on the rear of the wooden frame for hanging on a wall. The case should also have brass turnbuckles on the back to facilitate removal of the mounting board for close examination of the medals or rearrangement of the displayed items.

The mounting board is absolutely critical. Velvet, flannel and old uniforms, just don't do the job. A first class mounting system starts with acid-free Befang or Gator board at least 1/4 inch thick. This board is very sturdy, being composed of two layers of hard, white paper board sandwiched around a foam core. Over this, a high quality velour-type material to which velcro will adhere is glued and pressed down evenly. The medals are mounted using velcro tape; one piece over the ribbon mounting pin and one, about the size of a nickel, on the medal back. The velcro locks the medal very firmly into place without causing any damage and alleviates the need to cut off the pin backs. Badges or ribbon bars with pin backs can be mounted by pressing the prongs through the fabric into the gator board, which moulds around the prongs. A little velcro tape on the back of the pronged device adds extra holding power.

Patches, brass plates, dog tags and other mementos can easily be added this way. The great beauty of this method is found not only in its eye appeal, but also that one can add to the display or rearrange the existing contents by gently peeling the medal off as simply as opening a velcro zipper. Prong devices can also be moved easily, since the foam core closes in behind the prong as it is removed, thus effectively sealing the hole once more.

The final element in the process is the frame itself. While oak and other heavy woods make very handsome pieces of furniture, they are not a good choice for a frame. The frame's weight puts a great strain on modern  plasterboard walls when an extensive medal display is attached via standard hooks and nails. In addition, handling a heavy frame by very young or very old hands increases the chance it could be accidentally dropped. For these reasons, frames should be milled from a lightweight wood with good staining characteristics. Bass wood is considered the best for the purpose and some poplar is acceptable. Metal frames, on the other hand, should be avoided, owing to their heavy weight and to the bright coloring which can conflict with the patina of the medals. Finally, the wood stain, (e.g., walnut stain), should reflect a rich, warm glow to properly envelop and enhance the medal display.

An essential part of the display case is the brass plate which provides the key information pertaining to the recipient of the displayed awards. A high quality brass plate with good quality engraving will forever enhance the dignity of the medal display.

Whenever possible, the engraved letters should be blackened to provide enhanced contrast and visibility.

JOHN F. SCOTT
G CO, 2ND BN, 2ND MARINES
2ND MARINE DIVISION
FEBRUARY 1962 - AUGUST 1964

The plate should, as a minimum, contain the full name, assigned unit and time frame. Other useful items are rank, service number and branch of the service if space permits. The contents of a nameplate are obviously a personal preference, but experience has shown that a limit of four or five lines can enhance and compliment the display, while greater numbers are a distraction.

On the next page are some examples of different display cases. The Korean War display below has a cap insignia at the top with sergeant's chevrons centered. Displayed below the chevron's are the ribbons of the Navy Presidential Unit Citation and the Navy Unit Commendation. The medals, from left to right, are: The Marine Corps Good Conduct Medal, the National Defense Service Medal, the Korean Service Medal and the United Nations Service Medal (Korea).

Below the unit citation ribbons is a brass name plate with the Marine's name and service information. The plate is flanked by Rifle Sharpshooter and Pistol Expert badges.

World War II

The 2ⁿᵈ Marine Division Patch is topped by an Officer's Cap Insignia and flanked by Captain's Rank Insignia. The Medals shown are: Bronze Star, Purple Heart, American Campaign, Asiatic-Pacific Campaign, WWII Victory, Navy Occupation and the 50th Anniversary of WW II Medals. Marksmanship Badges and an Honorable Discharge Pin (ruptured duck) are displayed adjacent to a name plate.

Pacific Service

A Marine Blazer Emblem is flanked by Corporal's Chevrons and Dress Collar Insignia. The Medals Shown are: Bronze Star, Purple Heart, Good Conduct, American Defense, American Campaign, Asiatic-Pacific, WWII Victory and 2 Commemorative Medals. A name plate is flanked by Marksmanship Badges.

Korean Service

Dress Collar Insignia and the 1ˢᵗ Marine Division Patch are displayed above the Good Conduct, National Defense Service, Korean Service, UN Korean Service and Korean Service Commemorative Medals. Displayed below are the Navy and Korean Presidential Unit Citations above a name plate and Marksmanship Badges.

Vietnam Service

Rank Cap Insignia are displayed above the Bronze Star, Purple Heart, Navy Commendation, National Defense Service, Vietnam Service, RVN Civil Actions, RVN Campaign Medals and a Commemorative Medal. The Combat Action Ribbon and Navy PUC are shown above a name plate and Marksmanship Badges.

Peacetime Service

Rank and Cap Insignia are displayed over Ribbons and Medals. The Medals are: Navy Achievement, Good Conduct, National Defense Service, Armed Forces Expeditionary, Armed Forces and Humanitarian Service and UN Medals. The Ribbon set also includes the Sea Service and Overseas Service Ribbons, which are ribbon only awards.

Southwest Asia Service

A Marine Medallion and Dress Collar Insignia are displayed above Ribbons and Medals. The Medals are: Navy Achievement, Good Conduct, National Defense Service, Southwest Asia Service and Saudi & Kuwait Liberation Medals. The Ribbon set also includes the Sea Service and Overseas Service Ribbons, which are ribbon only awards.

Claiming Medals From the U.S. Government

Veterans of any U.S. military service may request replacement of medals which have been lost, stolen, destroyed or rendered unfit through no fault of the recipient. Requests may also be filed for awards that were earned but, for any reason, were never issued to the service member. The next-of-kin of deceased veterans may also make the same request.

Requests pertaining Marines should be sent to:

Navy Liaison Office (Navy Medals)
Room 5409
9700 Page Avenue
St. Louis, MO 63132-5100

It is recommended that requesters use Standard Form 180, Request Pertaining to Military Records, when applying. Forms are available from offices of the Department of Veterans Affairs (VA). If the Standard Form is not used, a letter may be sent, but it must include: the veteran's full name used while in the service, approximate dates of service, and service number. The letter must be signed by the veteran or his next of kin, indicating the relationship to the deceased.

It is also helpful to include copies of any military service documents that indicate eligibility for medals, such as military orders or the veteran's report of separation (DD Form 214 or its earlier equivalent). This is especially important if the request pertains to one of the millions of veterans whose records were lost in a fire at the National Personnel Records Center in 1973.

Finally, requesters should exercise extreme patience. It may take several months or, in some cases, a year to determine eligibility and dispatch medals.

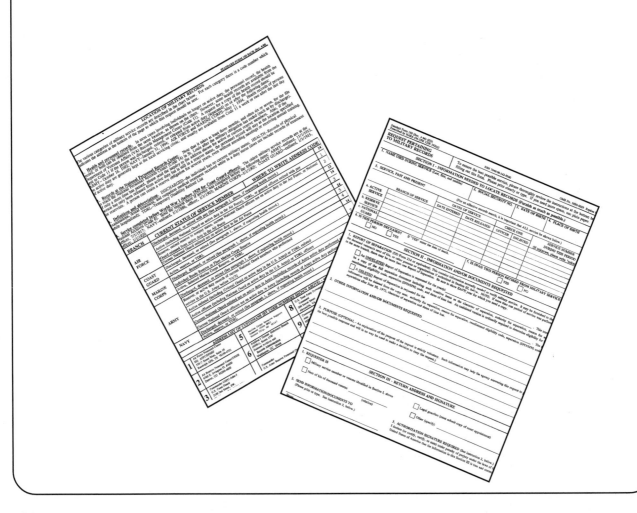

Commemorative medals have been struck for centuries to celebrate specific events. Several countries even struck official state commemorative medals authorized for wear. As the United States has developed a tradition rich military history, commemorative medals have begun to appear. *(Commemorative medals are not authorized for wear on the uniform.)*

50th Anniversary of World War II Victory Medal

The 50th Anniversary of World War II Victory Medal was struck to commemorate and honor veterans of World War II. It is appropriate for all World War II veterans and if displayed should be the last medal displayed.

The reverse of the medal has the Official 50th Anniversary logo. It is an appropriate medal for all military personnel who were awarded the World War II Victory Medal.

The Korean War Service Commemorative Medal

The Korean War Service Commemorative Medal has a complex history. In 1954 (after the armistice was signed) the Government of South Korea established a War Service Medal for those who served in the conflict and offered it to all the United Nations Forces who served Korea. While some countries accepted the medal, the United States chose not to authorize it for wear on the uniform.

The Korea War veterans groups are working with Congress to get the medal accepted and for the Korean government to re-offer it. The commemorative medal was designed to very closely resemble the original medal and it was struck by one of America's leading manufacturers as "The Korean War Service Commemorative Medal" for Korean War veterans.

Wearing of Medals, Insignia and the Uniform by Veterans and Retirees

One of the first lessons taught to new recruits is proper wear of the uniform and its insignia. The same principle applies to the wearing of military awards by veterans and retirees. There are a number of occasions when tradition, patriotism, ceremonies and social occasions call for the wear of military awards.

Civilian Dress

The most common manner of wearing a decoration or medal is as a lapel pin, in the left lapel of a civilian suit jacket. The small enameled lapel pin represents the ribbon bar of a single decoration or ribbon an individual has received (usually the highest award or one having special meaning to the wearer). Many well-known veterans such as former Senator Bob Dole, a World War II Purple Heart recipient, wear a lapel pin. Pins are available for all awards and some ribbons such as the Combat Action Ribbon or the Navy Presidential Unit Citation. A small Marine Corps insignia and miniature wings are also worn in the lapel or as a tie tac. Additionally, retirees are encouraged to wear their USMC retired pin and World War II veterans are encouraged to wear their Honorable Discharge Pin (affectionately referred to as the "ruptured duck").

WW2 Honorable Discharge Pin

Honorable Discharge Pin

Retirement Pin

Honorably discharged and retired Marines may wear full-size or miniature medals on civilian suits on appropriate occasions such as Memorial Day and Armed Forces Day. It is not considered appropriate to wear marksmanship badges on civilian attire.

Formal Civilian Wear

For more formal occasions, it is correct and encouraged to wear miniature decorations and medals. For a black or white tie occasion, the rule is quite simple: if the lapel is wide enough wear the miniatures on the left lapel or, in the case of a shawl lapel on a tuxedo, the miniature medals are worn over the left breast pocket. The center of the holding bar of the bottom row of medals should be parallel to the deck immediately above the pocket. Do not wear a pocket handkerchief.

Miniature medals can also be worn on a civilian suit at veterans' functions, memorial events, formal occasions and social functions of a military nature.

Uniform

On certain occasions retired Marine Corps personnel may wear either the uniform prescribed at the date of retirement or any of the current active duty authorized uniforms. Retirees should adhere to the same grooming standards as Marine Corps active duty personnel when wearing the uniform (for example, a beard is inappropriate while in uniform). Whenever the uniform is worn, it must be done in such a manner as to reflect credit upon the individual and the corps. (Do not mix uniform items.)

The occasions for wear by retirees are :
- military ceremonies.
- military funerals, weddings, memorial services and inaugurals.
- patriotic parades on national holidays.
- military parades in which active or reserve units are participating.
- educational institutions when engaged in giving military instruction or responsible for military discipline.
- social or other functions when the invitation has obviously been influenced by the members having at one time been on active service.

Honorably separated wartime veterans may wear the uniform authorized at the time of their service.

The occasions are:
- military funerals, memorial services, and inaugurals.
- patriotic parades on national holidays.
- any occasion authorized by law.
- military parades in which active or reserve units are participating.

Non-wartime service personnel separated (other than retired and Reserve) are not authorized to wear the uniform but may wear their medals.

Wearing Medals, Ribbons, Badges and Insignia
(Text taken directly from Current Marine Corps Uniform Regulations)

<u>Full Size Medals</u> - Marines may wear up to four medals side by side on a 3 ¼ inch bar. A maximum of seven medals may be overlapped (not to exceed 50% with the right or inboard medal shown in full). Full size medals blue or white dress jacket centered on the left breast pocket with the upper edge of the holding bar on line midway between the 1st and 2nd button of the jacket. When large medals are worn, all unit citations and ribbons with no medals authorized are centered over the right breast pocket the bottom edge 1/8 inch above the top of the pocket.

For men, the maximum width of the holding bar for large medals is 5-3/4 inches, and the length of the medals from top of holding bar to bottom of medallions is 3-1/4 inches. A maximum of four large medals side by side will fit on the maximum width of holding bar; however, a maximum of seven medals will fit on the holding bar if overlapped. The overlapping on each row is equal (not to exceed 50 percent). The right or inboard medal shows in full.

Women wear no more than three large medals side by side on a single holding bar not to exceed 4-1/4 inches; however, a maximum of five medals will fit on the holding bar if overlapped.

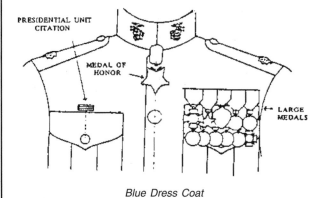

Blue Dress Coat

The Medal of Honor is worn around the neck with the ribbon under the coat or jacket collar of the officer's evening dress and all other dress "A" uniforms. The medallion is hung one inch below the bottom edge of the collar. On the officer/SNCO mess dress and the SNCO evening dress uniform, the Medal of Honor is worn around the neck with the ribbon under the jacket collar. The medallion hangs one inch below the bow tie.

<u>Miniature Medals</u> - On the evening dress jackets miniature medals will be centered on the left front jacket panel midway between the inner edge and the left armhole seam, with the top of the bar on line with the 2nd blind button hole. On mess and SNCO evening and mess dress uniforms, the miniature medals are centered on the left lapel with the top of the holding bar 1 inch below the lapel notch. When miniature medals are worn, no ribbons are worn.

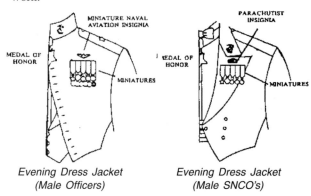

Evening Dress Jacket   *Evening Dress Jacket*
(Male Officers)   *(Male SNCO's)*

1. For men, the maximum width of the holding bar for miniature medals is four inches, and the length of the medals from the top of the holding bar to the bottom of medals will be 2-1/4 inches. A maximum of five miniature medals side by side will fit on a 4-inch holding bar; however, a maximum of ten medals will fit on the holding bar if overlapped. The overlapping on each row is equal (not to exceed 50 percent). The right or inboard medal shows in full.

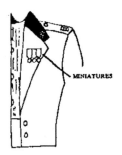

Evening Dress Jacket
(Female)

2. For women, the holding bar for miniature medals is no wider than 3-1/4 inches. A maximum of four medals side by side will fit on this width holding bar; however, a maximum of eight medals will fit on the holding bar if overlapped.

Miniature medals may be worn with civilian evening dress. If the medals are worn they should be worn centered on the left lapel, placed horizontally and one inch below the collar gorge. If a second row of miniatures are worn, it should be placed one inch below the first row. No more than two rows of miniatures should be worn on civilian attire.

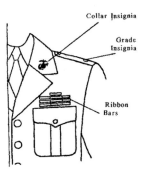

Service Coat

Service Ribbons - On uniform coats ribbons are normally worn in rows of three or four when displaying a large number of awards. If the lapel conceals any ribbons they may be placed in successively decreasing rows (ie: 4,3,2,1). All aligned vertically on the center, except if the top row can be altered to present the neatest appearance. Ribbon rows may be spaced 1/8 inch apart or together. When marksmanship badges are worn, the ribbon bars are 1/8 inch above them. Marines wear all ribbons to which they are entitled on service and dress "B" coats. Ribbon only awards are worn on the dress "A" coats above the upper right pocket when full size medals are worn over the upper left pocket.

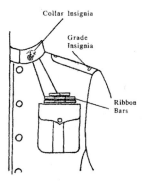

Blue Dress Coat

1. When the blue dress "C"/"D" or service "B"/"C" uniforms are worn the wearing of ribbons on khaki shirts is at the individual's option unless the commander prescribes that ribbons be worn. If ribbons are worn on these uniforms, either all ribbons, or personal U.S. decorations with U.S. unit awards and the Good Conduct Medal, may be worn at the individual's option.

2. Ribbon bars are worn on a bar or bars and pinned to the coat or shirt. No portion of the bar or pin is to be visible.

3. Two-ribbon rows may be worn by female Marines when a three-ribbon row would not lay flat or would extend too close to the armhole seam.

4. When more than one row of ribbon bars is worn, all rows except the uppermost are to contain the same number of ribbons. If the number of ribbons worn causes the ribbons to be concealed by the service coat lapel (one-third or more of a ribbon concealed), ribbon bars are to be placed in successively decreasing rows; e.g., 4-ribbon rows, 3-ribbon rows, 2-ribbon rows, single ribbon. The left (outer) edge of all decreasing rows are to be in line vertically; except that when the top row presents an unsatisfactory appearance when so aligned, it is to be placed in the position presenting the neatest appearance (usually centered over the row immediately below it).

5. On women's coats with horizontal pockets, ribbons are to be worn as prescribed above. On women's coats with slanted upper pockets, a horizontal line tangent to the highest point of the pocket will be considered the top of the pocket. On women's khaki shirts, ribbon bars are to be placed even with or up to two inches above the first visible button and centered so that they are in about the same position as when worn on the coat. On the maternity tunic, ribbon bars are to be placed so that they are in about the same position as when worn on the service coats. On the khaki maternity shirt, when worn as an outer garment, ribbon bars are to be worn in the same manner as on the standard khaki shirt, except they are to be placed 1/2 to one inch above the horizontal yoke seam stitching and may be adjusted to the individual to present a military appearance.

Civilian Clothing - Medals, ribbon bars, or lapel pins may be worn on civilian clothes at the individual's discretion. Individuals should ensure that the occasion and the manner of wearing do not reflect discredit on the award. Honorable discharge buttons, retirement buttons, FMCR buttons, rosettes and ribbon bar lapel buttons may be worn in the button hole on the left lapel of a civilian coat (see page 106).

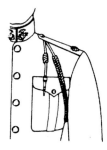

Blue Dress Coat

Fourragere - Marines entitled to wear the Fourragere will wear it on all uniform coats and jackets when medals and ribbon bars are prescribed. The Fourragere is worn over the left shoulder with the left arm passing through the large loop of the cord; the small loop will attach to the button of the shoulder strap and the metal pencil attachment will hang naturally to the front.

Service Coat

Aiguillettes - Service aiguillettes will be fastened under the shoulder strap and go around the shoulder just under the armpit, with the longest loop nearest the collar. On the khaki shirt, service aiguillettes will go around the shoulder just under the armpit, with the longest loop nearest the collar, and fastened at the shoulder just inside the armhole seam. Aides to the President, Vice-President, foreign heads of state, and aides at the White House will wear aiguillettes on the right shoulder. All other aides will wear aiguillettes on the left shoulder.

Dress aiguillettes are worn on the evening dress, blue dress "A"/"B", blue-white dress uniforms. Both plaited cords and the front single loop are worn in the front of the arm, the rear single loop passing from the rear under the arm.

Evening Dress Jacket

1. Men. On the evening dress jacket, dress aiguillettes worn on the right side will be suspended from a hook at the inside at the base of the collar closure; those worn on the left side will be suspended from the top button. The shoulder straps on the evening dress jacket may be modified, at the individual's option, to allow the aiguillette to pass under the shoulder strap as depicted in figure 4-2. Dress aiguillettes will be suspended from the top button of the blue dress coats.

Evening Dress Jacket
(Female)

2. Women. On the evening dress jackets and blue dress coats, dress aiguillettes will be suspended from the milled nut securing the branch of service insignia or from a small button attached to the body of the jacket/coat under the extreme inside point of slash between lapel and collar on the side on which the aiguillette is worn.

Marksmanship Badges - Badges are worn, according to seniority, centered above the left breast pocket, with the bottom edge of the highest holding bar 1/8 inch above the pocket's top edge. Unless otherwise prescribed by a commander, wearing marksmanship badges is at the option of the individual. Up to three badges may be worn, but no more than one for any weapon should be worn. Marksmanship badges are not worn with evening dress, blue dress "A" and utility uniforms.

Cap Insignia - Dress cap insignia is worn with the dress cap, centered vertically in the eyelet provided. When the service frame cap is worn with service uniforms, service cap insignia is worn centered vertically in the eyelet provided. It is also worn in the same manner on the fiber sun helmet and campaign hat.

The left service collar insignia is worn on the left front side of the garrison cap, with the insignia centered vertically in the eyelet provided.

Collar Insignia - Dress collar insignia is worn on the blue dress coats and evening dress jackets placed in the eyelets provided, with eagles facing inboard, as follows:

1. For male personnel, on the blue dress coats and the officers' evening dress jacket; the insignia is aligned vertically in the center of each side of the collar. On the SNCO evening dress jacket the insignia is worn on each side with the wing span horizontally parallel to the deck.

2. For female personnel, on the evening dress jacket and the blue dress coats, the insignia is worn on each side centered between the crease roll and edge of the collar, with the wing span parallel to the bottom edge of the coat or jacket.

Service collar insignia is worn on the collar of service coats, centered on the collar in the eyelets provided, eagles facing inboard, with the wing tips parallel to the bottom of the coat.

Officers' Rank Insignia - Metal insignia with clutch-type fasteners are worn on all uniforms except for evening dress jackets. Evening dress jacket insignia are embroidered and stitched on the shoulder strap. Metal insignia are worn on the shoulder strap and shirt collar as follows:

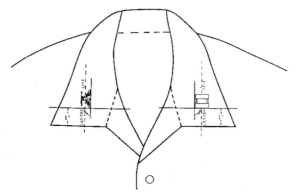

Short Sleeve Khaki Shirt

1. All officers wear their rank insignia so that it is equidistant from the front and rear edges of the shoulder straps. Collar grade insignia is worn on both sides of the collar of khaki shirts and utility coats. The collar insignia is centered between the top and bottom edge of the collar, with the outer edge of the insignia one inch from the front edge of the collar. Collar grade insignia is also worn on the right side of the garrison cap, opposite the branch of service insignia.

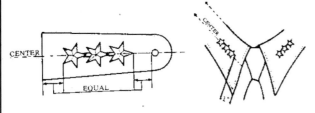

Lieutenant General

2. General officers' shoulder stars are worn equally spaced between the arm hole seam and the shoulder strap button. One ray of the star points toward the collar. General officers' collar stars are worn with one ray pointing toward the top edge of the collar. Collar stars are worn on the garrison cap, with one ray of each star pointing to the top of the cap with the long axis horizontal.

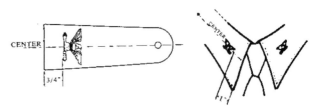

Colonel

3. Colonels' shoulder eagles are worn with the wings at right angles to the center line of the shoulder strap with the eagle's head toward the collar and facing front. Colonels' collar eagles are worn with the eagle's head toward the top of the collar facing the front, with the wings perpendicular to the front edge of the collar. A collar eagle is worn on the garrison cap, with the head facing forward.

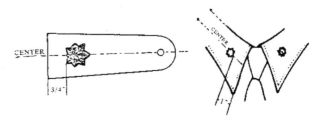

Lieutenant Colonel and Major

4. Field grade shoulder oak leaves are worn with the stem toward the arm hole seam. Field grade collar oak leaves are worn with the stem toward the bottom of the collar and the line from the tip to the stem parallel to the front collar edge. A collar oak leave is worn on the garrison cap, with the stem toward the bottom of the cap.

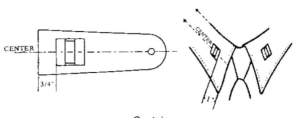

Captain

5. Company grade shoulder bars are worn with the long axis of the bars at right angles to the center of the shoulder strap. Company grade collar bars are worn with the long axis of the bars parallel to the front edge of the collar. A collar bar(s) is worn on the garrison cap with the long axis of the bar(s) essentially vertical.

6. Those warrant officers officially designated as "Marine Gunner" wear the Marine Gunner insignia. The Marine Gunner shoulder insignia is a replica of a bursting bomb. The insignia is worn on both shoulder straps of the dress coat/jacket. The burst of the bomb faces inboard, parallel to the sides of the shoulder strap with the center bottom of the sphere 3/4 inch from the inboard edge of the grade insignia.

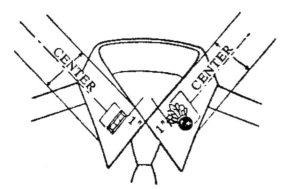

Warrant Officer/Marine Gunner

The miniature service insignia is worn on the left collar point of khaki shirts and utility coats. The insignia is centered one inch from and parallel to the front edge of the collar with the burst of the bomb toward the top edge of the collar.

Enlisted Cloth Rank Insignia - Cloth insignia is available in two sizes, large for men and small for women. Insignia is sewn on garments with thread that matches the background material of the insignia using a straight machine stitch. Insignia is worn single point up, centered on the outer half of each sleeve. Insignia will be placed four inches below the shoulder seam (three inches for male First Sergeant/Master Sergeant and above).

1. Green on scarlet insignia is worn on green service coats.

2. Green on khaki insignia is worn on khaki shirts. On short sleeve khaki shirts, insignia is centered between the shoulder seam and the bottom edge of the sleeve (men) or the peak of the cuff (women).

3. Standard gold on scarlet insignia is worn on blue dress coats and female SNCO's evening dress jackets.

4. Washable gold on scarlet insignia is worn on women's (blue dress) white shirts, centered between the shoulder seam and the peak of the cuff. However, they are no longer required.

5. Distinctive 1890's style gold on scarlet insignia is worn on the male SNCO's evening dress jacket, placed three inches below the shoulder seam.

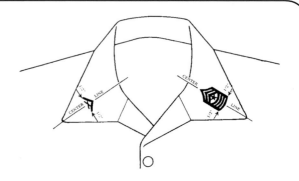

Lance Corporal   *Sergeant Major*

Enlisted Metal/Plastic Rank Insignia - Black metal/plastic insignia is worn as indicated below:

1. AWC, field coat, utility coat and maternity work uniform coat; vertically, on each side of the collar with the single point up and the center of the insignia on a line bisecting the angle of the point of the collar. The lower outside edge of the insignia is equally spaced 1/2 inch from both sides of the collar.

2. Khaki shirt; only when the service sweater is worn, in the same manner as above.

3. Tanker jacket; insignia is worn on each shoulder strap, single point inboard, and placed so that it is equidistant from the front and rear edges of the shoulder straps with the lowest point of the insignia's outer edge 3/4 inch from the armhole seam.

4. Camouflage Extended Cold Weather Clothing System (ECWCS) parka; one insignia is worn centered on the zipper flap in the space provided.

5. Organizational clothing (cover-alls, food service uniforms, aviation clothing, etc.); insignia is worn, in the same manner as worn on the utility coat.

Service Stripes - Service stripes are worn on the outer half of each sleeve of dress/service coats; gold on scarlet on the blue dress coat and green on scarlet on the green coat. Service stripes are placed at a 30 degree angle to the bottom of the sleeve. The first stripe will be placed as follows:

1. Blue dress coat; lower scarlet point of the stripe meets the point of the piping of the cuff.

2. Green service coat; lower scarlet edge of the stripe centered 1/2 inch above the point of the cuff.

3. Succeeding stripes are 1/8 inch above and parallel to the next lower stripe.

4. Service stripes are not worn on the AWC, tanker jacket or on the SNCO evening dress uniforms.

Rank Insignia and Service Stripes
(Male)

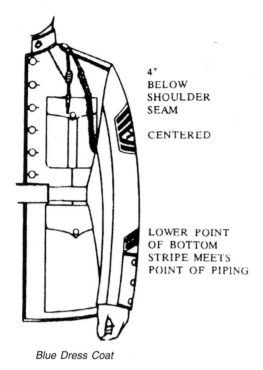

4"
BELOW
SHOULDER
SEAM

CENTERED

LOWER POINT
OF BOTTOM
STRIPE MEETS
POINT OF PIPING

Blue Dress Coat

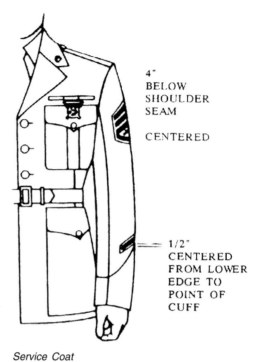

4"
BELOW
SHOULDER
SEAM

CENTERED

1/2"
CENTERED
FROM LOWER
EDGE TO
POINT OF
CUFF

Service Coat

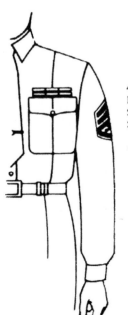

4"
BELOW
SHOULDER
SEAM

CENTERED

Long Sleeve Shirt

CENTERED BETWEEN SHOULDER
SEAM AND BOTTOM EDGE
OF SLEEVE

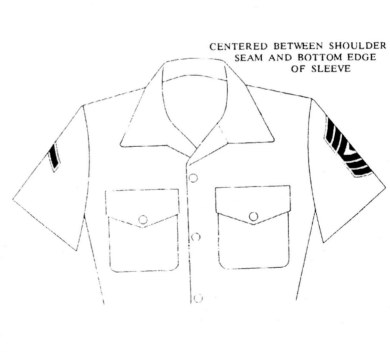

Short Sleeve Shirt

Rank Insignia and Service Stripes
(Female)

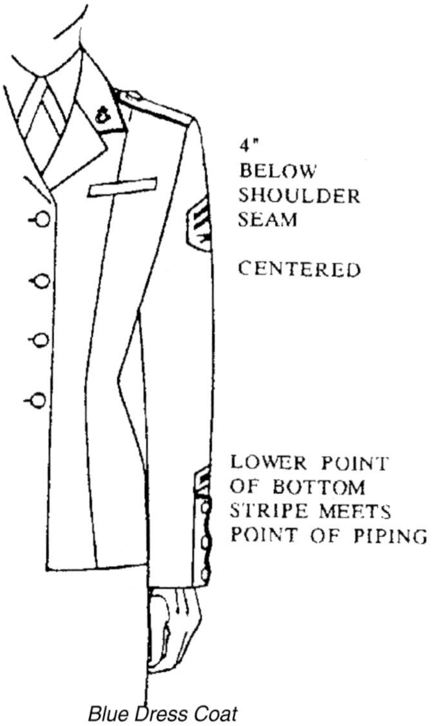

4"
BELOW
SHOULDER
SEAM

CENTERED

LOWER POINT
OF BOTTOM
STRIPE MEETS
POINT OF PIPING

Blue Dress Coat

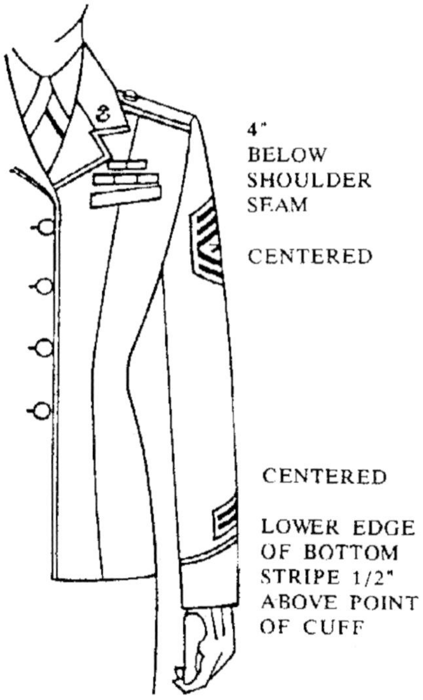

4"
BELOW
SHOULDER
SEAM

CENTERED

CENTERED

LOWER EDGE
OF BOTTOM
STRIPE 1/2"
ABOVE POINT
OF CUFF

Service Coat

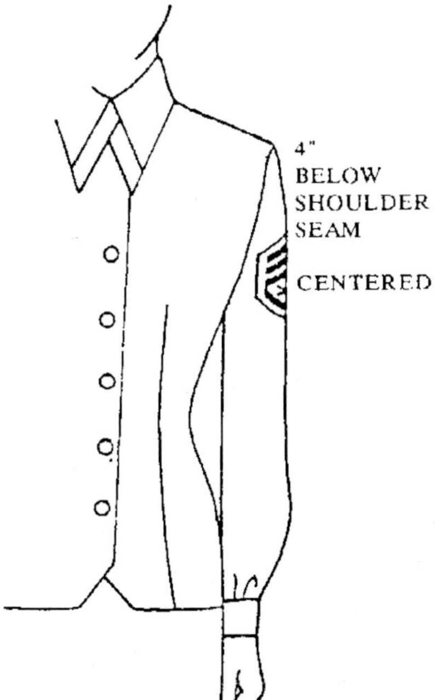

4"
BELOW
SHOULDER
SEAM

CENTERED

Long Sleeve Shirt

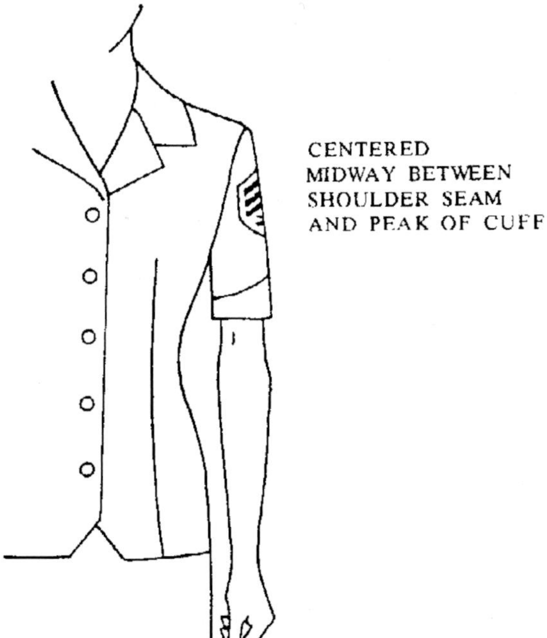

CENTERED
MIDWAY BETWEEN
SHOULDER SEAM
AND PEAK OF CUFF

Short Sleeve Shirt

Placement of Breast Insignia, Ribbons and Badges

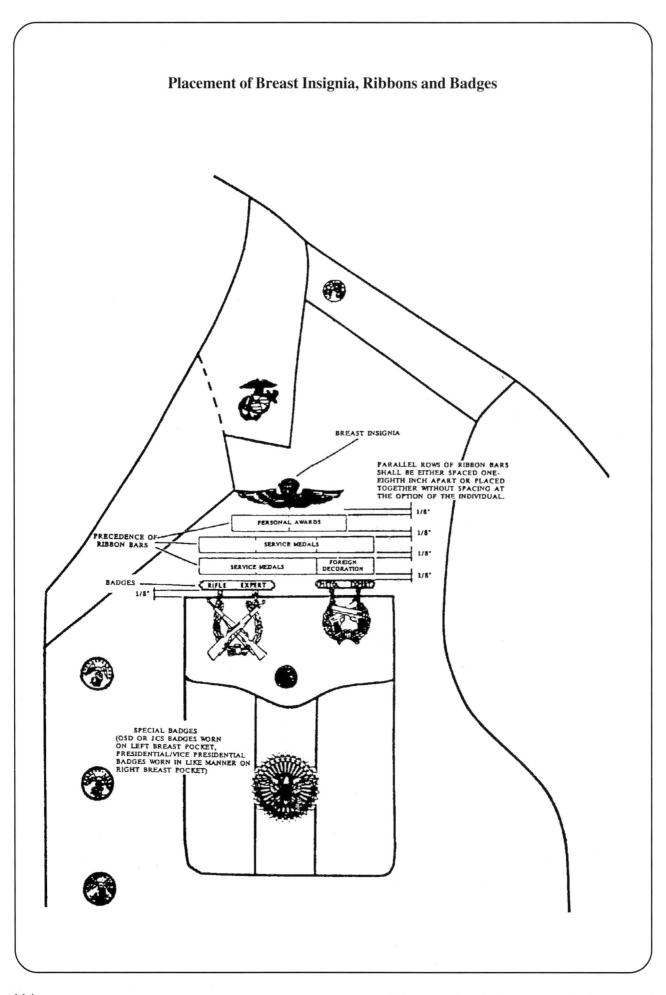

BREAST INSIGNIA

PARALLEL ROWS OF RIBBON BARS
SHALL BE EITHER SPACED ONE-
EIGHTH INCH APART OR PLACED
TOGETHER WITHOUT SPACING AT
THE OPTION OF THE INDIVIDUAL.

1/8"

PERSONAL AWARDS

1/8"

PRECEDENCE OF
RIBBON BARS

SERVICE MEDALS

1/8"

SERVICE MEDALS

FOREIGN
DECORATION

1/8"

BADGES

RIFLE   EXPERT

1/8"

SPECIAL BADGES
(OSD OR JCS BADGES WORN
ON LEFT BREAST POCKET,
PRESIDENTIAL/VICE PRESIDENTIAL
BADGES WORN IN LIKE MANNER ON
RIGHT BREAST POCKET)

Breast Insignia - Authorized insignia is worn on the left breast of all service and dress coats. It may be worn at the individual's option on khaki shirts worn as the outer garment (with or without ribbons), utility coats or the maternity work uniform coats. Miniature insignia, one-half regular size, is worn on evening dress jackets. Breast insignia is not worn on the cloak/cape, AWC, tanker jacket, field coat or sweater. When breast insignia is worn on the dress coat, service coat, khaki shirt, or maternity tunic, the insignia is placed with wings horizontal and parallel to the top of the breast pockets (if any). On women's coats with slanted pockets, a horizontal line tangent to the highest point of the pocket is considered the top of the pocket.

1. When worn alone, the insignia is worn in the same position a single ribbon would be worn.

2. When worn with medals, ribbons, or membership badges, the bottom of the insignia is centered 1/8 inch above the top row of such awards. When successively decreasing rows of ribbon bars are worn, and the top row of ribbons is such that centering the insignia presents an unsatisfactory appearance, the insignia may be centered between the outer edge of the coat lapel and the left edge of the vertically aligned ribbon rows.

3. When worn on the camouflage utility coat, the bottom of the insignia is centered 1/2 inch above the service tape.

4. When worn on the camouflage maternity work uniform, the bottom of the insignia is centered 1/2 inch above the service tape.

5. When worn on male officers' evening dress jacket, the miniature insignia is placed on the left front panel on a line 1/8 inch above the second blind buttonhole, and spaced midway between the inner edge and left armhole seam.

6. When worn on evening dress jackets with lapels, the miniature insignia is centered 1/8 inch above the miniature medals, or if no medals are authorized, the miniature insignia will be centered on the lapel at the position prescribed for the top of the medal bar.

7. Other U.S. service pilot/navigator insignia or foreign pilot insignia earned while the individual was a member of the foreign or other U.S. service may be worn provided the insignia is a duly authorized qualification insignia. These insignia may be worn on the right breast, in the same manner as Navy/Marine Corps insignia are worn on the left breast.

8. Other U.S. service pilot insignia earned as a Marine while undergoing training leading to qualification for the naval aviation insignia is worn on the left breast as prescribed above, until qualified and authorized to wear the Naval Aviator insignia, at which time the other service insignia is no longer worn.

9. When two Navy/Marine Corps aviation insignia are worn at a time, the senior insignia is worn 1/8 inch above the other as follows (from top to bottom):
   (a) Naval Aviator and Naval Aviation Pilot
   (b) Naval Flight Officer
   (c) Marine Aerial Navigator
   (d) Naval Aviation Observer
   (e) Combat Aircrew
   (f) Naval Aircrew

However, a Marine qualified for both naval aircrew and combat aircrew insignia wears only the one of his/her choice.

10. When the Navy/Marine Corps parachutist insignia is worn, the basic parachutist insignia is not worn. When aviation insignia is worn with the basic or Navy/Marine Corps parachutist insignia, the parachutist insignia is centered 1/8 inch above any aviation insignia.

11. When EOD insignia is worn with aviation or parachutist insignia, the EOD insignia is centered 1/8 inch above the other insignia.

12. When SCUBA diver insignia is worn with any other breast insignia, the scuba diver insignia is centered 1/8 inch above the other insignia.

13. Not more than two USMC-approved breast insignia will be worn on the left, and not more than one foreign pilot or other U.S. service pilot/navigator insignia will be worn on the right, at any time.

Service Identification Badges - The Presidential Service Badge (PSB), the Vice-Presidential Service Badge (VPSB), the Office of the Secretary of Defense Identification Badge (OSD ID Badge), and the Joint Chiefs of Staff Identification Badge (JCS ID Badge) are authorized to be worn on Marine Corps uniforms and can be worn after detachment from qualifying duty.

No more than two service/identification badges are worn on the same side of the uniform. When two badges are worn, they are worn vertically aligned on the upper pocket or corresponding position on uniforms which do not have pockets in this position. On pockets which have flaps, these badges are vertically centered between the lower point of the flap and bottom of the pocket, midway between the two sides. When both the PSB and VPSB are worn, the PSB is uppermost. If both OSD and JCS badges are worn, the OSD is uppermost. If an OSD or JCS badge is worn with a command identification device, the OSD/JCS badge is uppermost. On women's coats and khaki shirts, the lower badge is placed similar to a single badge with the second badge worn centered 1/8" above the first.

The ID badges are worn centered on the upper right pocket, or corresponding position on the uniforms which do not have a pocket in this position. These badges are not worn on the AWC, tanker jacket, service or blue dress sweaters, or utility uniforms.

A miniature ID badge may be worn on the evening dress, blue dress "C"/"D," and service "B"/"C" uniforms. Placement is as follows:

1. Male officers' evening dress jacket; the badge is placed on the left front panel with the top of the badge centered one inch below the bottom edge of the miniature medals.

2. Male SNCO's evening dress jacket; the badge is placed on the left front panel on an extension of an imaginary line formed by the three front buttons of the left panel. The badge is placed midway between the top button and the point where the imaginary line meets the lapel.

3. Female officers' and SNCO's evening dress jacket; the badge is placed centered on the left front panel with the bottom of badge about two inches higher than the top button. The placement of the badge may be adjusted slightly to ensure the proper flat appearance.

4. Men's khaki shirts; the badge is worn centered on the left pocket.

5. Women's khaki shirts; the badge is worn on the left side centered 1/8 inch above the top row of any awards (i.e. ribbons, breast insignia, marksmanship badges) worn. If awards are not worn, the badge is centered on a horizontal line even with or up to two inches above the first visible button from the top.

Long before we wear the uniform, long before the eagle, globe, and anchor is etched in our soul - - we sense the special character that sets Marines apart. Silent to the ear - - Marine ethos, values, and character speak to the nation's heart. They say more about who we are than the dignity of our uniforms, the pageantry of our parades, or the inspiration of our hymn. The nation expects her Marines to be the world's finest military professionals. The nation demands that her Marines be forever capable and ready, rich in history and traditions, and instilled with the traditional virtues - - honor, courage, and commitment - - that demonstrate we remain faithful. In short, we must deserve the nation's trust.

—— General Charles C. Krulak, Commandant of the Marine Corps,
from "Ethos and Values,"
Marine Corps Gazette, November 1996

Placement of Devices on Ribbons and Medals

No. of Awards	3/16 Bronze and Silver Campaign Stars	Bronze Letter V	Humanitarian Service Medal	Air Medal Individual	Air Medal Strike Flight
1		V		★	1
2	★	★ V	★	★	2
3	★ ★	★ V ★	★ ★	★ ★	3
4	★ ★ ★	★ ★ V ★	★ ★ ★	★ ★ ★	4
5	★ ★ ★ ★	★ ★ V ★ ★	★ ★ ★ ★	★ ★ ★ ★	5
6	★				
7	★ ★				
8	★ ★ ★				
9	★ ★ ★ ★				
10	★ ★ ★ ★ ★				

Campaign Medal

Bronze Star Medal

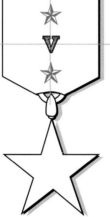

Humanitarian Service Medal

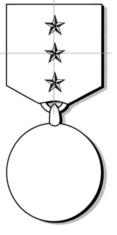

Armed Forces Reserve Medal

After 10 years of reserve service

With 1 mobilization

With 2 mobilizations

After 10 years of reserve service and 3 mobilizations

Air Medal

Occupation Medal

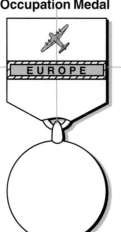

Armed Forces Reserve Medal

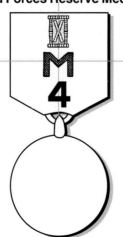

The Young Marines of the Marine Corps League

The Young Marines is the official "action" youth program of the Marine Corps League of the United States. The organization is for ages eight through high school and the focal point for the Marine Corps Youth Drug Demand Reduction Program. Its mission is to promote the mental, moral, and physical development of young Americans. All of its activities emphasize the importance of honesty, courage, respect, loyalty, dependability, and a sense of devotion to God, country, community and family.

The Young Marines were organized in 1958, and became a chartered subsidiary of the Marine Corps League. In 1980, the organization became a separate corporation and was granted status as a youth educational organization with an IRS classification of 501C3. In 1993, the Commandant of the Marine Corps officially recognized the Young Marines with MARINE CORPS ORDER 5000.20. The purpose of the order stipulated: "To officially recognize the Young Marines of the Marine Corps League; to identify the Young Marines as the focal organization for the Marine Corps drug demand reduction efforts; and to promulgate Marine Corps policy for support of the Young Marines."

The Young Marines currently have 151 units with over 8,000 members and their future goal is 200 units with a membership of 12,000 by 1998. Members meet weekly throughout the year and are led by adult volunteers who are carefully screened based on background information and recommendations. Many of the volunteers are off-duty Marines, who willingly give their time to this great program.

The Emblem of the Young Marines is a badge of Marine Corps red and gold. The center of the badge is blue with the Marine Corps Monument depicting the flag raising on Suribachi Yama, Iwo Jima, in gold. Between this and an outer ring is a gold laurel wreath and the words YOUNG MARINES are placed at the top, M. C. L. and the Marine Corps Emblem at the bottom bracketed by gold laurel branches.

Similar to the Marine Corps, the Young Marines utilize an Awards Program that recognizes and motivates (see page 56). Awards are classified into three categories:

1. Personal decorations are bestowed upon an individual for specific act(s) of gallantry or meritorious service.

2. Service awards are issued to an individual in recognition of achievements accomplished in a creditable manner, or participation in designated events.

3. Qualification awards are issued for satisfactory completion of prescribed courses of instruction.

For more information contact:
Young Marines National Headquarters
P.O. Box 70735
Southwest Station
Washington, D.C. 20024-0735

Belden, B.L.- *United States War Medals*, 1916

Blakeney, J.- *HEROES U.S. Marine Corps 1861-1955*, 1957

Borthwick, D. and Britton, J.- *Medals, Military and Civilian of the United States*, 1984

Borts, L.H. and Foster, F.C.- *United States Military Medals 1939 to Present*, 1995

Borts, L.H.- *United Nations Medals and Missions*, 1997

Campbell, B.L. and Reynolds, R.- *Marine Badges of the World*, 1983

Davis, R.G. - *The Story of Ray Davis, General of Marines*, 1995

Dorling, H.T.- *Ribbons and Medals*, 1983

Fowler, W. and Kerrigan, E.- *American Military Insignia and Decorations*, 1995

Gliem, A.F.- *United States Medals of Honor 1862-1989*, 1989

Kerrigan, E.- *American Badges and Insignia*, 1967

Kerrigan, E.- *American Medals and Decorations*, 1990

Kerrigan, E.-*American War Medals and Decorations*, 1971

Kerrigan, E.-*Guidebook of U.S. Medals*, 1994

Lelle, J.E. -*The Brevet Medal*, 1988

McDowell, C.P.- *Military and Naval Decorations of the United States*

Miller, Z.- *Corps Values*, 1997

Morgan, J.L. and Thurman, Ted A. - *American Military Patch Guide,* 1997

National Geographic Society- *Insignia and Decorations of the United States*, 1944

Rosignoli, G.- *Badges and Insignia of World War II*

Rosignoli, G.- *The Illustrated Encyclopedia of Military Insignia of the 20th Century*

Rottman, G.- *US Marine Corps 1941-45*, 1995

Russell, L.E.- *The US Marine Corps since 1945*, 1984

Selby, J.- *United States Marine Corps*, 1972

Smith, Richard W. - *Shoulder Sleeve Insignia of the U.S. Armed Forces 1941-1945*, 1981

Strandberg, J.E. and Bender, R.J.- *The Call to Duty*, 1994

Sylvester, J. and Foster, F.C. -*The Decorations and Medals of the Republic of Vietnam and Her Allies,* 1995

Thomas, G.C., Heinl, R.D., and Ageton, A.A.- *Marine Officer's Guide*, 1956

U.S. Marine Corps- *Battle Skills Training/Essential Subjects Handbook*, 1989

U.S. Marine Corps Order P1000.6 - *Assignment, Classification, and Travel Systems Manual (ACTS Man.)*

U.S. Marine Corps Order P1020.34F- *Marine Corps Uniform Regulations*, 1988

U.S. Marine Corps Historical Division- *United States Marine Corps Ranks and Grades 1775-1969*, 1969

U.S. Navy Instruction SECNAVINST 1650.1F- *Navy and Marine Corps Awards Manual*, 1991

U.S. Navy Manual NAVPERS 15,790- *Decorations, Medals, Ribbons and Badges of the United States Navy, Marine Corps and Coast Guard, 1861-1948*, 1 July 1950

Vietnam Council on Foreign Relations- *Awards and Decorations of Vietnam*, 1972

Visconage, M.D.-*U.S. Marine Corps Marksmanship Badges from 1912 to the Present*, 1982

INDEX

Notes

MEDALS of AMERICA
EST. 1972

In 1993 Medals of America Press published its first book on the U.S. Military Awards, *United States Military Medals 1939 to Present*. It became an immediate American institution selling over 50,000 copies. Since then MOA Press has become the acknowledged expert and foremost publisher on United States Military and Allied awards.

Readers and purchasers of these information-packed award books come from the 28 million military veterans, their families, active duty and reserve troops, collectors, military buffs, researchers, historians, libraries, museum shops, catalog houses and book stores. This growing series of beautifully illustrated and written books tell the secrets, history, beauty and unravels the mystery of the medals, the insignia and badges that honor the military service of American men and women.

Written, illustrated and photographed by America's leading authorities, the books are part of a growing series of timeless information, illustrations and remarkable color photographs of America's military awards and insignia. To order call Medals of America or visit our web site @ www.usmedals.com

Medals of America　　　　Telephone: (800) 308-0849
1929 Fairview Road　　　Fax:　　　(800) 407-8640　Overseas Fax: (864) 862-7495
Fountain Inn, SC 29644　　Web:　　　HTTP://WWW.USMEDALS.COM

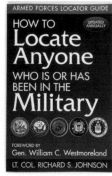

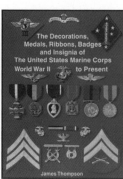
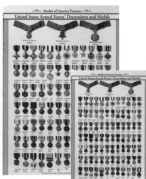